The First **Time I . . .**

1.350

D0590124

9/9/ B/

The First Time I . . .

Edited and Illustrated

by

The Hon. Theodora Benson

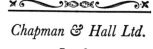

Chapman & Hall Ltd.

London

First published

1935

CHAPMAN & HALL LTD.

11 Henrietta St.

LONDON

W.C.2

Printed in Great Britain by The Whitefriars Press Ltd., London and Tonbridge,
and bound by A. W. Bain & Co., Ltd., London

CONTENTS

v

Contents

ILLUSTRATIONS

Illustrations

The First Time I went Horse-racing

by

LOUIS GOLDING

I

IT was in Berlin that I first went horse-racing. But there was a time before the first time. Yet I cannot say I *went* on that occasion, any more than you can say, when you get into bed : " I am going to dream " ; any more than you can go to a musical-comedy and say : " I am going to fall in love with a chorus-girl."

It is important about that experience in Doomington that I did not actually go horse-racing, so much as that horse-racing befell me, as Wordsworth's daffodils befell him. It is a long time ago now, and it was on a Saturday. I conclude it was a Saturday, for these two reasons. Earlier that same phantasmal day I had been praying by my father's side in the synagogue. That would indicate it was either a feast-day, which might fall upon any day of the week, or a Saturday. On those days I would go beside him to morning prayer, he in his silk hat, I in my bowler. He thought it would be disrespectful to Jehovah if I wore any hat less ceremonious than a bowler when I presented myself to His notice. The bowler would lie about my forehead like a circlet of hot steel. My ears would be scarlet with the shame of my bowler. I would drop a pace or two behind him, and remove the bowler from my head, in the hope that the passer-by might imagine that my connection with the bowler was of the most casual. I fingered it airily, inconsequently, as if it were a roll of newspaper. My father would turn round and fix me with his earnest and suffering eyes. I would replace the bowler upon my head and, bowed down under the weight of it, shuffle along the pavements to the synagogue two or three corners away from Strangeways Gaol.

It was a synagogue day, therefore either a Saturday or a feast-day. But it was late in the year, it was November. I remember that the trees, when at last I got out to them, had few leaves on them, or none. The air was laced with grey mist. Now it happens that I am aware that for these three last years, at least, the November Handicap has been run on a Saturday. It all hangs together. On a certain Saturday over three decades ago, I went forth from the synagogue wearing a bowler hat, I went forth like a sleep-walker, I beheld enchanted beasts running, with enchanted humans poised on their backs as lightly as harebells are poised on their stalks . . . it was the November Handicap I fell upon, the November Handicap !

I say I went forth like a sleep-walker. Certain less abstracted ones among the elders must have looked on me curiously, the small pale boy, with his hands fluttering slightly before him, threading his way among the praying-shawls. Others, my father amongst them, had no eyes for me. Their eyes were turned inward upon the awful contemplation of I-am-that-I-am. For me there had been enough praying, enough beating of bosoms for sins real or fancied. I arose from my place on the hard form alongside the Ark of the Law, I went down into the Doomington Road, and set my forehead in the direction where, a long way away, there were meadows. The trams clanged beside me, but I did not hear them. I went forth past the Jewish shops that were shut because it was the Sabbath, past the Gentile shops that were open because it was a weekday. I came to a region where I believed Earls and Countesses lived, because there were houses here with gardens to them. I came to a place where the road swept round upon itself like a cutlass. I descended a sort of terrace and found myself against a wall just too high for me to look over it.

I had a sense that there was a descending hillside below the wall, and the green floor of a valley. There would be trees there, too. I climbed upon a milestone and swung myself on to the broad coping of the wall. The breath was arrested in my throat. I gazed into a wider, greener, waterier world than I had suspected, across a sweet smokeless curtain of grey rain. The raindrops condensed upon the fringe of my forehead. There was a river curled round in the valley, and though I must have realised intellectually that it was none other than the River Irwell which flowed so sluggishly, or did not flow, through the heart of the town, between mills and warehouses as black as itself, to me it seemed it was at one and the same time all the mythical rivers they told me of in the geography lesson—Rhine and Severn, Tiber and Danube and Nile.

I sat there on the damp coping of the wall, kicking

13

the bricks behind me with my heels, and suddenly started singing. It was not the mournful singing of the old men I had left behind me in the synagogue, beating their breasts, nor the mechanical singing of the singing-lesson at the Board School, where in a mosquito-like chorus we commended the virtues of the Roast Beef of Old England. It was tuneless, toneless, wordless, but there was glory in it.

And then slowly, like the condensed raindrops falling from my forehead, the sounds tumbled from my lower lip, slowly, then more slowly, till there were no more left at all. I saw a vision. I saw it as movement first, then as colour, then at last I resolved it into its elements. It was a long low loping movement, lovelier than birds, because it had a regularity in its rhythm which birds lack. I had not yet seen the sea, but I imagined that the waves so pursue each other to the land. Then came the perception of colour, pink, white, green, yellow, chocolate, maroon above, on the bases of dappled grey and chestnut and strawberry roan, all these dimmed and subtilised across the interposed mist. By now I had perceived and separated the elements of the enchantment, the riders, the race-horses, princes respectively of the two-footed and four-footed spheres.

The movement continued, green and white overtook maroon, and was overtaken by black and primrose. Then the leaders swerved round the far barriers and I could see them no more. Now at last the whole field was gone, even to the last laggard. I sat on the coping, no longer kicking the brick wall with my heels. I had no song to sing. I felt the

rain coursing gently down my spine. I had seen the
horse-races ! I had seen the horse-races ! It was
unspeakably pagan and impious. What would those
others think or say, swaying under the shadow of the
Ark of the Law ! It was lovely ! It was lovely !
How should I express the impiety and the loveliness ?

I seized the bowler-hat with my right hand,
caved it in with my left fist, gazed at it for one
moment in malevolence and triumph, then flung
it as far from me down the hillside as those thin
biceps could fling, as near to the conquering hooves
as it might be. Had I not seen the horse-races ?

II

That happened a long time ago. Years passed
by and it frequently seemed it had not happened
at all. It formed part of a mythical world, like
tiger-hunting in Nepal or pearl-fishing in the Sandwich Islands. I had not gone horse-racing on that
dream-occasion, as I have been at pains to make
clear, it had merely happened to me. As the years
went on it never for one moment occurred to me
that I might deliberately go to some race-course
and renew that early ecstasy. For one thing, New-
market or Lingfield, or even the race-course on the
Irwell where the November Handicap is run, seemed
quite as far from the sort of person I was and the
sort of associates I had, as Nepal or the Sandwich
Islands. And then I realised more and more
clearly that the horse-racing you might of set purpose
go and look at could have no relation with the
experience I had had that day. A great deal of
horse-racing seemed to happen a long way away

from the race-courses—in public-houses and at street-corners where anxious men with waterproof collars consulted the stop-press news.

I developed, in fact, a determination that I would not go horse-racing, even if the chance fantastically presented itself, for fear of the outrage that it might be upon the memory of my exquisite experience. Yet in this place I must confess that before I actually went horse-racing in Berlin, I did in fact attempt to go horse-racing in London. And that was not because I had lost sight of my secret resolve. It was because I had learned to drive a motor car. The day upon which I had happened to learn to drive was the day before the Derby. From what I am about to relate, it will be evident I had not learned to drive very efficiently. When Derby Day dawned, it occurred to me that I would like to take a young lady for a drive, partly for the pleasure of her company, partly to show off my new accomplishment. And seeing that it was Derby Day, it was decided we should drive to the Derby. I will not elaborate the nightmare of that journey. The journey, in fact, proceeded no further than Richmond Hill. I found myself a cog in a slowly moving chain, a cog which jerked and started and stopped without any reference to the suave complex chain in which it found itself involved. I remember at one moment a certain toughening of the noises beneath the bonnet of the car. I had a dim memory that this was the contingency against which the manœuvre called getting into second gear was provided. I got into second gear and reversed statelily into a magnificent Daimler. The driver of the Daimler left his wheel. He came slowly up to me and with the most searing gentleness apologised to me. That was the crisis of the attempt I made that Derby Day to go horse-racing. The young lady at my side masterfully dislodged me and took the wheel. She negotiated us into some unexpected bay on Richmond Hill. When the cavalcade of cars had defiled at length, she turned the bonnet of the car down-hill again, and homeward. As we slid skilfully along the greasy tram-lines of the Chiswick High Road, it seemed to me that I would sooner lie on a nailed plank like a Hindoo fakir than make the attempt to go horse-racing ever again.

III

And then I went to Berlin. And then at last I went horse-racing. This was in the early summer of 1931. I went to the horse-races at Grunewald, and I went there meaning to get there. I did not attempt to get there in my own car, for I did not have a car (and I do not propose to have one, either). Nor did I go in the special char-a-banc that took you out for a few pfennigs. I went out in a hired limousine. Seeing that I could not by any possible chance lose on the six o'clock was I the one to boggle at a hired limousine? I would never have forgiven myself for my meanness. Besides, little Helmut (let me call him that) was with me. It was Helmut who had put me on to *Imperator*. Could I possibly let him come out horse-racing with me in a mere taxi?

This account of how I finally went horse-racing is partly a tale of little Helmut, partly a tale of my conscience. And the lamented Edgar Wallace has quite a lot to do with it, too. Little Helmut was little because he used to be a jockey. I did not know that till the day he called on me in my room. He and his wife lived in the obscure tail-end of the apartment where I was lodging in Berlin. I, having become a literary gentleman, had a forward room that looked across the Spree through a lovely green tangle of tree-tops. I had a good view of the suicides which were attempted daily by those disheartened Berliners, and were sometimes frustrated.

I had often wondered when Helmut's turn would come. (I did not know his name till the day he called on me.) He seemed so forlorn and unnecessary, the way he wandered in at all hours of the day and night. His wife did not look happy either. Who would, with Helmut for husband? (And you know what that name means? *Hell Mut*—Bright Spirit! Very odd!)

The day before he called on me Helmut had asked me for a cigarette. Not a mere match, mark you. A cigarette. I felt pretty certain that that meant the opening up of pourparlers. I was right. The next day I met him at the front door. He had doubtless been waiting for me a long time. He said " Shush ! " and put his finger to his mouth. I looked behind me apprehensively. " Herr Professor," he whispered, " do you want to win a lot of money ? "

What is the instinctive answer to that question? " Yes ! " I said.

" Then, Herr Professor, may I come into your

room and speak to you a few minutes ? " I was not certain that his mode of address was happy.

" Forgive ! " I said. " I am no Herr Professor. Come this way ! " He sat down. " What is it all about ? "

" Will you put fifty pounds, one thousand marks, on a horse that cannot lose ? "

" Fifty pounds ! " I cried in terror. " There is no such sum of money ! "

" Hush ! " he bade me again. " Fifty pounds ! What is fifty pounds to you ? A literary gentleman ! What is fifty pounds to Herr Ed-garr Vall-ass ? "

" I'm sorry," I said curtly, " I'm not interested in horse-racing. It's not my line ! " I did not tell him of the November Handicap long long ago. I did not even recall it. It belonged to a pre-existence in another planet.

He looked shocked and incredulous. " But you **are** an Englishman ! You come from sport-land ! You must not speak so ! "

I tried to point out to him that sport and putting money on things are not interchangeable terms. Whereas I brandish my tennis-racket with the next man, I told him, and have been known to kick the greasy football, I just did not put money on horses.

" But Herr Ed-garr Vall-ass," he pointed out. " He owns race-horses. He too was once a jockey. But he made more money out of his books. So now he runs horses instead of riding them. *Nicht wahr ?* "

I tried to suggest that Herr Vall-ass and modern English literature were not synonyms. But, in company with some millions of Germans, he refused to believe it. I am less familiar with the German best-sellers of a later *régime,* but in those days Mr. Wallace was read in Germany a good deal more than Goethe, or, I should think, any German writer, dead or living. His long cigarette-holder protruded elegantly from every book-shop window and book-stall in the country. " *Es ist unmöglich von Edgar Wallace nicht gefesselt zu sein,*" read the caption on millions of volumes.

That was how Helmut got me first. He made me feel that if I did not fall in with his ideas, I would be unworthy of my craft, I would be letting Herr Vall-ass down.

" What do you know about horse-racing ? " I said, trying to bluster.

" I ? I am an ex-jockey ! " I had never met a jockey past or present. I was thrilled, but tried not to show it. He had put a lot of weight on since his jockey days. But I could begin to understand now why he wandered about in that neglected-looking way. " I tell you," he went on, " it is quite impossible for you to lose ! "

I put on my most man-of-the-world manner. " Really ! You mustn't tell me tales of that sort ! *Blödsinn !* Nonsense ! What do you mean, quite impossible to lose ? "

" Don't you understand, Herr Doktor ? It's all arranged. Or it'll all be arranged in two hours. We *know* what horse is going to win ! The others won't win ! They'll not be allowed to ! "

" What ! " I cried. " You want me to mix myself up with dirt like that ? I'm sorry ! You've

come to the wrong shop ! Well, I've got to get on
with my work——"

" Herr Doktor," he implored. " I want you to
understand. It is impossible for German racing to
go on unless every third race is cooked like that.
I am not speaking of the big events. It is the understood thing. It is not dishonest. It is the way that
owners make their expenses. Do you know how
much the upkeep of a horse costs these days ?
And the stables ? And the trainers ? " He reeled
off an enormous list of figures. I have always been
susceptible to figures. It did seem as if nobody
could make any money unless a little money was
made on the side. " And is it my business, anyhow,
the way the people behind the scenes manage these
things ? " asked Helmut. He was giving me a tip
. . . a horse that couldn't lose. He wasn't asking
me to sit on any horse and hold him from winning.

" What interest to you is it," I asked, " to give
me an inside tip ? I have the honour to live in the
same house as you. Beyond that I don't know you."

" I'll be quite frank with you. My chance of
earning a living comes when my own particular
friends arrange a race like this. I ask for thirty per
cent. of the winnings." Then he added magnani-
mously : " I only take thirty per cent. after your
original stakes are restored to you." Somehow that
touch impressed me greatly with his *bona-fides.*

" What horse is it ? " I asked.

" I cannot tell you," he said, " yet. I am going
off to the lads shortly. Then we decide."

" What races, then ? "

" You will understand, Herr Doktor, I can say no

21

word. Not until I have your fifty pounds in my hand."

" Fifty pounds ! " I snorted. " *Wurst !* How am I to know that your story is true—about all your jockeys sitting in counsel together ? "

" Can I trust you ? " He eyed me sombrely.

" I am a literary gentleman ! " I reminded him.

" Well, you can come down with me. We are meeting in the Zentral Hotel in the Friedrichstrasse one hour from now."

Suddenly a quite automatic spasm of nausea arose in me. My gorge rose at the whole shoddy business. " I'm sorry. I'm busy. I must really get down to it. Good-bye ! "

Then Helmut played his trump card. He suddenly reached forward and seized my two hands. His eyes were moist with tears. " You have seen my wife ? " he said.

I said, " Yes."

" You have not noticed ? "

" What ? " I asked.

" But that she is ill, she is so ill ! "

" I am sorry ! " I said briefly.

" She has an illness on the kidneys, Herr Doktor. She needs another operation. The last one was a failure. I paid for it with my commissions on the last race with which my group of jockeys was tied up. I would back my last pfennig on them to-morrow. Her life depends on it. But I have no pfennig." His voice quivered. The hard edges of my heart dripped like an icicle in a thaw. Had I the right to condemn the poor little woman to a premature grave? And her husband to an inconsolable widowhood? Was I such a Pharisee?

I tried to make my voice as gruff as I could. I tried to show myself as downy as they make them. "What odds?"

"I can promise you a clear eight to one!"

"I'll put fifty marks on!"

"You will! You will! *Fabelhaft!*" His eyes shone. I realised I could easily have got away with five. But would his 30 per cent. on five marks at eight to one pay for the operation? It would not. "I'll give you a receipt at once!"

"No!" I said. "We'll go down to the Zentral Hotel first. Then I'll make up my mind."

So we went down to the Friedrichstrasse.

"Listen!" he said. "You must come in a few minutes after me. We'll be in the *Herrenzimmer*. Sit down quite casually at a table near me!"

The thrill of all that was worth the money. What had Vall-ass in his myriad equestrian pages to compare with it? I followed him a few minutes later. Yes, there he was. There they all were—about nine jockeys and one ex-jockey. They didn't look quite human, but they didn't look like horses either. One of them had a face like Charles Peace as a Young Man. A debased version of Mr. Charles Laughton was also present. I ordered a half-and-half and opened a Continental *Daily Mail* as if I were not a mysterious figure in a racing thriller. Oh, yes, they had their heads together. There was argument this way and that. Now and again I heard a queer distortion of an English word emerge from their whispered babel of dialects . . . "*odts*,"

" *shtrate* "—*i.e.*, odds, straight—and so on. Helmut paid no more attention to me than if I were a table.

We met late that night. We arranged to leave for Grunewald next day.

" What is the name of the horse ? " I whispered.

" No ! " he said. " I'll tell you when we set off to-morrow. I daren't breathe it to-night. If the lads heard about it——" He made the gesture as of a knife slitting a throat.

" I understand ! " I breathed.

I met him in a passage of our house at two-thirty next day. Under each arm he bore an enormous parcel of asparagus for his sick wife. I cannot describe how that charmed me. It did more than that. It reassured me. I had had a nasty moment or two overnight regarding my fifty marks. But how could you believe there was anything shady about a gentleman who bought his sick wife two packets of asparagus in advance out of his hard-earned commission ?

We set off at about four. The races began at three. I learned from Helmut that people like ourselves, in the upper swim of horse-racing society, do not turn up for the first race or two, like the mere rabble. It was a comfortable limousine, and fairly expensive. I was going horse-racing. At last I was going horse-racing. We were held up for a moment outside a smart hatter's. The window was full of the most exemplary grey hats and green hats and black bowlers. Suddenly, from out of infinitely submerged depths, a profound sense arose to me of the unfitness of my headgear.

MR. LOUIS GOLDING AT GRUNEWALD.

" Stop ! " I cried to Helmut. " Tell the chauffeur
to stop ! "

" What is it ? " asked Helmut, startled.

" I will be back in one moment ! " I cried. I
went into the smart hatter's and took off my decayed
trilby. " Send this to my house ! " I bade. " Find
me a bowler, it must be of the best quality ! "

I returned to the car. I smiled at Helmut.
Helmut smiled at me.

" What is the name of the horse ? " I asked behind
my hand, so that the chauffeur should not hear.

" *Imperator !* " he whispered.

" Ha ! " I said.

Grunewald is one of the most beautiful race-
courses in the world. The races were, I do not doubt,
good races, but neither the horses nor the jockeys
were quite so lovely as those I had once glimpsed
through a curtain of grey rain. I quite failed to
make up my mind which of the races were *shtrate*
and which were not. The fact was, I could hardly
breathe till our race came on—my race, Helmut's
race, Imperator's race. The six o'clock got under
way at length.

" There, there ! " Helmut muttered through his
teeth. " That's him ! Dark blue with a red cap ! "

" Ha ! " I said. My knees were knocking with
excitement. The race started. They were all of a
bunch for a little way. They thinned out. Imperator was running fourth. Imperator was running
third. " Hi ! Hi ! Hi ! " I shrieked as one does,
when one has fifty marks on at eight to one, with a
rebate of 30 per cent. for commission. " Hi !
Hi ! " I could not decide whether it was more

intolerable to look or not to look. Imperator was running second. No, he could *not* get the lead, he *could* not! My heart thumped against the larynx. *Herr Gott!* He was gaining. He was gaining! They were neck and neck. He was leading. My eyes could not stand it. They closed.

I had seen such a lovely Gothic madonna on the Kurfurstendamm! I should be able to buy it now. I would bring a posy of orchids for Frau Helmut. Dear Frau Helmut—the operation will put things right for you! I opened my eyes. A totally new phenomenon had thrust itself forward. A fiend of a dappled grey was nosing forward, fast, faster. The jockey. . . . Was it? Yes, it was! The jockey with a face like Charles Peace as a Young Man! He was running a fierce second. He was gaining! He was gaining!

I looked at Helmut. He tore his hair. He shook his fists. He gabbled something in German. It was clearly the word for "double-crossed." His mouth twisted frightfully.

Imperator came in third actually. Charles Peace was an easy first.

There would be no orchids for Frau Helmut. I sighed. "I am so sorry!" said Helmut, with a break in the voice. "I am so sorry, Herr Doktor! But listen!" He bent towards me. "We've got to get our own back. I can't possibly allow you to be down like this! Now on Sunday, at Ruhle- ben——"

Suddenly my heart turned over inside me like a motor-car engine. "Stow it!" I said unpleasantly. I looked round. "I wonder," said I to myself,

" if there are a lot of literary gentlemen here who put a bit on Imperator ! I wonder ! "

I removed the bowler-hat from my head with my right hand, and caved it in with my left fist, then I threw it as far as I could throw it, among the press of feet. When I reached home, I had a word or two with the landlady. She informed me that Frau Helmut's kidneys were as sound as a bell, so far as *she* knew. But she eats too much asparagus, she said.

The First Time I took a Holiday

by
HOWARD SPRING

THE holiday stands out in my mind as a bright foreground, but you will understand nothing about the foreground unless you know something of the background too.

It was not a drab background, but it was one of startling opportunism. You took what you could get when you could get it, and it didn't work out badly. If there was no long stretch of joyous freedom by the sea or in the hills to which you could look back and say : " That was my holiday ! " there were at any rate rare jewels of days threaded here and there along the string of the year, and they made a gleaming handful to count over in a dark time.

There was the waifs' and strays' outing, as we called it, though we were not precisely to be reckoned in either category. We were just very poor children whose parents snatched anything they could for their offspring, and the outing to Barry Island was certainly a thing to snatch. I remember little of it, but chiefly the delirium of passing through the tunnel. Railway coaches were not lighted in those days. The sexes were segregated, God help us : little boys in one compartment, little girls in another ; but the partition did not go right up to the ceiling. You could stand on your seat and look over. And when you came to the tunnel you could do more. With a knotted handkerchief, a belt, or a cricket-stump, you could lash over blindly into the darkness, raising hell generally, and filling the tunnel, unfortunately brief, with demoniac uproar.

That, chiefly, I remember of the waifs' and strays' outing from Cardiff, our native city, to Barry Island : that and running on sand, and the persuasion, which lasted for years, that we had been " cut off by the tide " because we had waded some yards through rising water from a rock ; and tea and buns ; and a man with black formal clothes and a great power of producing a piercing whistle by putting two fingers in his mouth and blowing ; and giving at the end of the day, when we were all hot and tired and dusty, three cheers for God knows whom, and going home happy.

There was, too, the annual picnic of the Bible Class. Each year the power of God among us waxed in early June, to wane at the month's end. The graph of membership rose steeply, declined as sharply. The picnic was in mid-June.

We would betake ourselves with the paraphernalia of cricket and rounders to some meadow newly green from the year's haymaking, and there beguile a sunny hour or two till the moment came for the day's high peak : tea in a cottage garden. How well I recall one such occasion : the table of planks piled high with buttered scones, and cake richly brown, oozing currants, lashings of bread and butter, pineapple chunks and stewed pears ! Tea-urns sizzled at the table's head where sat the lame old man with silver hair who was our shepherd during

HAPPINESS.

these ungraceful ventures into the fold ; and all about were tall hollyhocks, and beehives of golden plaited straw, and the shrill call of swifts wheeling under the blue sky. And what added joy we felt in the security of that brief paradise when we perceived, gazing over the hornbeam hedge, one of our number who had turned his footsteps to the path of truth too scandalously late to deceive even the ingenuous shepherd who now, in a thin tenor voice, was leading us in the singing of our grace. " Praise God from Whom all blessings flow," we shrilly sang, and the face at the hedge disappeared as a sinner's might do who had been permitted, as torture's refinement, to peep upon angels at play.

And when life could not rise to such heights as these, there was always the improvisation of our own delights. In the long school holiday we would be up early and away into the dewy fields which lay then much nearer to the city than they do now, and we would seek mushrooms, though I do not remember that we ever found one, or gather the flat bunches of elderberries that stained the fingers an exciting purple, and from which our mother concocted wine. Or, making a whole-day job of it, we would set out with a few slabs of bread-and-butter and a bottle of water ; and in those unexacting days these simple provisions answered to all that we knew by the name of dinner. We took with us a book on natural history, and discovered much joy in identifying this and that ; and in a stream at Fairwater, crossed by a railway bridge whose embankment was at times like a long snowdrift, so thickly the dog-daisies grew there, we would fish by

37

the hour, tirelessly turning over the stones in search of millers' thumbs.

Once I wandered away from my brothers and sisters and went into a near-by field and right out in the middle of it I lay down in grass so high that no one could see me. The red sorrel from that angle rose like spires and the dog-daisies trembled against the blue with fantastic loveliness. The silence was so great that I could hear the grasses making a small commotion like the trees of a forest in which I was a beetle. I shut my eyes and tried to forget that I was anyone at all. I tried to imagine that I was a stone lying on the ground ; and I remember snatching myself up from what must have been something near to unconsciousness and rushing away frightened.

So in the summer we improvised our substitute for what other people called " holidays," and when the board school was again in session and we back at it, it would be not wholly with a sense of desolation that we heard other children speak of grand times they had had at Ilfracombe or Weston-super-Mare.

Nor were the winters without joyful occasions. There was an entertainment, known no doubt to those who organised it by some magniloquent title, which we called briefly " Santa Claus." Santa Claus was always held in a great hall in the centre of Cardiff. It was a feed, and an entertainment, and a bright new penny for each child, and as you left you were given a bag containing an apple and an orange and some cast-off clothing.

It doesn't sound great fun ; and I suppose that

to children whose Christmas entertainment is stalls at the pantomime and everything else to scale it wouldn't be great fun ; but Santa Claus remains all the same in my mind as a high light, a time of chewing and bawling, of gusty good humour, and the surprise of the sack which you lugged home to see what your mother's patient fingers could do with the garments it contained.

These were strange things from which to extract joy, but joy we found in them ; and, stranger still, there was joy to be found in the soup kitchen. In bitter winters the soup kitchen was opened in the fire station, and to get the soup thence was to me a fascinating experience. Tickets were supplied by the police, and armed therewith you could enter that mysterious and attractive place where all woodwork was a glowing red, and all metal work was twinkling brass, and the hoses were rolled like very tidy snakes who had washed themselves and coiled up for sleep. A grand place, full of all that cleanness and glitter, and beatified now with the incense rising from the steaming cauldrons of good pea soup !

What a long time I am getting to my first holiday ; but that's just it : I *was* a long time getting to it, and when it came it had all the enchantment of a complete experience after so many nibblings at the rind of joy.

There was an interregnum, a time when we were still too poor to go away for a holiday, but now too proud to take the bliss offered by Santa Claus and the Bible Class or anyone else who could give us something for nothing. This was perhaps the hardest time of all : the time of waking up to the good things that can be wrested from life while you are still too weak to do the wresting.

I do not remember in what year the first holiday came. I was sixteen or seventeen years old. My elder brother and I had been saving up for a long time, and at last a week's holiday could be achieved. We decided to go to Bideford because somebody we knew had been there and had given us the name of a sensationally cheap boarding-house. We had written and arranged to pay twelve-and-six a week each, to cover everything. We were to share a bed, but we had always done that, and had occasionally had other members of the family sleeping at the foot of it with their legs pushed up between us. So there was no hardship in sharing a bed.

But when we had saved the twelve-and-six each, and a few shillings each for expenses when we got there, the question remained of getting to Bideford.

Now it is one of the joys and the scandals of newspaper life that newspaper men can get many things for nothing. We were both working in a newspaper office, and the office possessed a pass which permitted free travel on the paddle steamers plying between Cardiff and Ilfracombe. We were allowed the use of the pass, but there still remained the railway journey from Ilfracombe to Bideford and back. My brother settled that heroically. " We'll walk it." It is something like twenty miles.

On a cloudless day of June we set out on that holiday. We had no appropriate clothes. We wore the stuffy city clothes that were all we had. Inexperienced travellers as we were, we had fantastic notions of the things we should need. It still is a bafflement to me, when I see a poor family going for a day at the seaside, to behold the meaningless things they take. All that we took with us that far-off June day was stuffed into a great tin portmanteau —food, overcoats, books, and God knows what— and in the brave spirit of youth we proposed to carry that portmanteau twenty miles !

Blue and lovely was the sea at Ilfracombe, darkening to green at the foot of Capstone Hill, grown so thick with valerian that a single sprig of the plant brings back the moment to me : the gulls wheeling and crying, and the paddles making a noisy frothy dither as we edged in to the pier as though over the effervescence of a colossal Seidlitz powder.

We humped that monstrous trunk ashore and then we ate the lunch that we had brought with us. We did not dream of spending our precious savings on restaurants. And when we had eaten we began to walk to Bideford.

It was about one o'clock, and the sun was at its powerful height. The noon of the day, and the noon of the year, that trunk, and twenty miles to go ! Now when I take a taxi to go a mile, I am not sure whether to be ashamed or to say : " By God, you've earned it ! "

We didn't carry that trunk to Bideford ! How could we have dreamed of doing it ? We were skinny strengthless boys. We did our best. We sweated along between hedgerows dripping with honeysuckle and ditches where the meadowsweet made a creamy foam. There were no tarmac roads then. Our shoes kicked up the pitiless dust.

We took turns with the trunk. We carried it at times between us. At times we dumped it and subsided into the hedge among the ragged robins and the foxgloves.

Never once did we complain. We were on our first holiday, and neither of us would admit that there was any flaw in the loveliness of the time we were having. No complaint, but at last from my brother a complete admission : " We can't do it."

It was true. We couldn't do it. We dumped the old trunk again and turned out our pockets. Each set aside his twelve-and-six and considered what was left. We could take the train, but it would mean that those small diversions we had promised ourselves must all be abandoned.

So on we went again till we came to the next village at which the train stopped. We had walked about ten miles. When we got to Bideford we carried the trunk up to our lodgings in a back street. A supper of shepherd's pie was waiting for us. It was brought in by a stout kind girl who said we looked very tired and that she hoped we would enjoy our holiday. We were tired. We went straight to bed by candle-light. Neither of us had ever spent a night away from home before, and that bare little bedroom in a quiet back street, with the candle-light flickering on a steel engraving of Jael driving the nail into the head of Sisera, seemed uncanny, cold and dubious. My brother read his Bible, as he always did at night right up to the time when he died soon afterwards on a ship at sea ; and I lay on my back looking across the thin outline

42

of his cheek against the yellow candle-shine to the dark eyes of Jael.

They haunted me all through the holiday, but we slept well because we were out all day. Long before breakfast the next morning we were on the quay, looking right towards the many arches of the lovely bridge and left towards the estuary. Behind us was the " Rose," the inn that has its place in " Westward Ho ! " and before us were the shining sands where Amyas Leigh fought his duel.

I had brought " Westward Ho ! " with me. I have never read it since, nor ever shall I. But I am prepared to defend it as a grand romance, let who say what he will. Every stone and tree, the pebble ridge on the near-by shore, the estuary sand and the boats in the river, all conspired to paint bright pictures that nothing can ever efface of Amyas and Salvation Yeo and all the others going about their high and mighty business.

No ; I do not want to read it again and I do not want to go to Bideford again. It is now a place in a dream, far off but very bright ; and I fear what I should find if I put it to the touch of waking. I should not find the tree in which I sat all through a summer day. We had taken food with us, and we found the tree on the edge of a field that was being mown. I climbed into it, and with my legs along a bough and my back to the trunk I read and read, peeping out through the leafy screen now to a blue vision of the estuary, now at my brother who was reading " Henry Esmond " at the tree's foot, now at the swarthy men whose scythes advanced with a rasping rhythm through the standing grass.

43

That afternoon I read in " Westward Ho ! "
" And beauty born of murmuring sound did pass
into her face," and that led me on to Wordsworth.

Of the brief holiday that day remains for ever, and
whatever modern villas may now adorn the hill,
my men for ever swing their scythes and my brother
reads on in a green shade.

Wherever our legs could take us we wandered
that week : out to Northam where, beneath grey
crooked stones, the graves of drowned mariners are
green ; to Appledore and Instow which come back
to me now, standing above the pearly iridescence of
the estuary at flood with the intangible grace and
mystery of a water-colour by Wilson Steer ; to the
old Army and Navy college which we found deserted
and open to any intruder. We looked about its
rooms, seeking on door or wall some scrawled
" R. K.," which might testify to the sojourn there
of Stalky's creator. But we found nothing.

All through the week we spent hardly a shilling,
but I doubt whether I shall ever again know a
holiday so mightily endowed with wonder and
refreshment. All too soon we were back. On my
way home from work each day thereafter I would
glimpse my face in shop mirrors, admiring its tan ;
then regretting that the tan was passing like the
holiday itself. Soon nothing was left—except this
which, long years after, I have been able to set down.

Since then, what holidays there have been !
But none like that. None which has left a place-
name so magic in my ears as Bideford is to this day.

Ah, les premières fleurs qu'elles sont parfumées !

*The First Time I Scaled the Heights of Nature—
and Plumbed the Depths of Human Nature*

by

WILLIAM GERHARDI

"THE FIRST TIME I SCALED THE HEIGHTS OF NATURE—AND PLUMBED THE DEPTHS OF HUMAN NATURE."

" . . . he thought how in reality, if one pondered deeply, all is beautiful in this world, all but what we think and do ourselves when we forget our human dignity and the higher aims of being."—*Tchehov.*

I

AT seventeen I travelled to Montreux. And, waking in the morning, suddenly I saw the mountains, for the first time in my life. The sun, like a warm blessing, lit the wide strip of water and kindled a memory in me of a state of well-being native and near to me, from which I had been sundered. When was it ? Where was it ? And above, inarticulate with the mystery, towered the mountains. My sleeper shot out of the tunnel into the light. And it was as though I who for so long had dwelt in twilight must at first avert my eyes as I came out into the light, into the morning. Into the morning !

The old life that had clung to me damply seemed to have tumbled to pieces like an old shell, a dried-up mould. I felt I was out, out of the narrow house, and could go where I liked, be what I liked. A blue, sunny sky stretched above me, trees fluttered in the breeze, and I went, stick in hand, over dell and hill without looking back. And the farther I

went the more clearly I understood that all these
things—myself—were but symbols and metaphors of
a miracle by whose dim candle I had read in the
book of life a sorry page, confused and deceptive :
and a nameless usher had closed the book and
carried it away " Yes," I thought, " I don't want
it. I don't want anything."

Yet I sat still, my mortal eyes resting on the unfolding space which opened out to right and left and
filled me with that mournful exultation peculiar to
man who looks at freedom through the windows of
a body which is not free.

II

I did not again come within visible distance of
mountains till, at the age of twenty-six, I went to
live in the Austrian Tyrol. Towards midday the
long, much-travelled, exhausted, dusty train from
Paris arrived at Kuffstein station. I drove in an
open cab, at first through the old mellow town with
its cloistered streets, domes, turrets, and pinnacles ;
then by the side of the river, angry and turbulent.
A faint hazy summer afternoon was drawing to its
close, and as, at sundown, I came to the hanging
bridge between rocks and the foaming green river
rushing angrily under the horse's hoofs, I looked at
it all with new awakened wonder, as if a little dazed
with rapture.

The *pension* at which I put up comprised two houses,
an old one like a Russian *datcha* inside, and a new
stone villa, with two rows of balconies practically
surrounding the house. I had the whole of the
middle balcony to myself, and both the balcony

48

and windows faced south. We were moderately high up, and were screened from the wind by enormously high mountains, north, east, and west, while towards the south the mountains were somewhat lower and occasionally a breeze came up a wide valley from Italy, *wo die Zitronen blühen.* . . . I sat there on the open balcony outside my room, and the view was magnificent. I could see the river, the beautiful turbulent Inn, and the bridges, I saw also the funicular going up the mountain slope, and all around were pine-trees, birches, roses, beautiful villas in lanes lined with foliage ; and at night when I walked by the river, where lanterns shone between secretive trees, I felt as though I were somewhere in China, in Peking. It was quiet ; I heard only church bells and the silvery sounds of cow bells. There were no motors, only horse carriages, and I could cross the street almost with my eyes shut : it was so quiet and slow, so neat and respectable.

There was only one other visitor in the *pension*, a thin, intense Englishwoman, violently pro-Bolshevik, anti-British, and a little unbalanced. I joined her at lunch, and she at once asked my advice as to how she could recover a trunk she had lent to some skunk of an English major who had since returned to England and was ignoring her letters. I said, " Write to Scotland Yard." She thanked me profusely. " Thank you, it is *so* kind of you. I'm very grateful *indeed*. I shall do so at once."

I went out and passed down the lane through the little Austrian village—pigs, roses, cottages, little children playing about, a hen crossing the road.

. . . There were inns in the hills. I wound my way up the Schillerweg and sat down in a beer garden, amidst the beer- and wine-drinking peasants, with chamois beards like shaving brushes stuck in their coloured hats, and the women in Tyrolese peasant dress, taken in tightly at the waist and showing off their figures to advantage, and sat still and looked down into the green folds of the valley and up at the jagged summits of naked rock. Fowls, chickens, strutted all over the place, jumped on the chairs. The little serving-maid, bare-legged, would call them : " *Zip-zip-zip !* " The sun, as if making a last effort, shone with a tragic brightness ; then, unable to sustain the effort, diminished its light. The bare-legged maid went in. When she came out she wore a pair of brown stockings. The sun set behind the hill and left the valley cold and un-friendly ; only the tips of rocks still gleamed in the sun. Far away, a train whistled, and then coiled below, like a serpent, on its long journey to Vienna. All the peasants, save for one old man, had already vanished down the hill. He drank his big mug to the bottom, smacking his lips. Having paid for the beer and lighted his pipe, he rose, and at once there came sounds of his jolly accordion, as, with twinkling eye, he strode to his own happy tune out of the courtyard. Fresh and alert, he went down the road making his own music, till his long curved pipe and his knapsack and the plume in his hat ducked by the hill, and only the jolly tune spoke of his fresh onward strides.

Mrs. Stanley awaited me for tea. An exceedingly thin, bony woman past middle age, her eyes peered at me tragically out of her sockets. By the shape of her features, her figure, her carriage, it was evident that she must have been a great beauty in her time. Now she looked somewhere round about forty-five. " It's perfectly scandalous ! " She had a shrill, scandalised air of speaking. " The Princess is seducing all the young men in the neighbourhood. What *will* the peasants think ! You know, when we drove off to Kuffstein this morning she was so jolly that I couldn't think what was the matter with her. She jumped and hopped and rolled in her seat and was all over the carriage. Then, at a very bad bump, her suitcase tumbled out on to the road and opened, and a bottle of brandy fell out and smashed. You know, I'm so stupid : even then it did not occur to me what it was that had made her so jolly. And she went on and she went on, and cursed the coach-man—cursed him and cursed him and cursed him like a common brawling woman. Perfectly disgusting ! And he, poor wretch, was patiently picking up the splinters out of the suitcase. I never saw anything like it. . . . I find the society in this *pension* literally appalling. An Irish adventuress married to a Russian prince cracked in the head, and everyone bowing and kowtowing before them. It's perfectly disgusting !

" My poor fool of a father was only a blooming baronet, and so I am nothing—nothing at all. But between you and me, with all these Whitechapel Jewesses calling themselves Russian princesses —why, she's only been married to Anton three months, and he was the illegitimate son of somebody-and-nobody—it's perfectly scandalous !—I felt I

simply had to call myself ' The Honourable.' They
like it here in the Tyrol, you know, though the poor
dears don't know what it means and think it's just
another Hochwohlgeboren.   Still, don't you think
I am entitled to it ? "

"Certainly . . . of course . . ." I propitiated
her.

"Thank you.   It's *so* kind of you.   I am *so* glad
you approve of my step.   Really, the spectacle of
all these people using titles to which they have not
the least right in the world makes one—I *so* hate
that feeling—a little bitter."

III

We sat on the balcony in the sun till it declined
towards evening, when suddenly the landscape
shone forth with a crystalline clearness, as though
you had adjusted your binoculars to the required
focus.   Tired of listening to Mrs. Stanley, I strolled
for hours through the pine-wood.   Suddenly the
sun came out again and shone through the trees
with a dazzling whiteness such as only acetylene
lamps can produce.   On the edge of the wood I stood
still ; below was a lake surrounded by firs : a little
lake, like a plum dipped in water.   Sky, firs, hills,
water, all was blue, each just a shade darker ;
all blue and motionless, as if waiting for something.
I stood still, my heart beating, till the sun sank, and
the first silver stars twinkled feebly in the sky.   I
walked on and on till the sky grew threadbare, the
moon paled, and a small peevish sun looked out,
sleepy, red-eyed.   Then a shaft of light licked a
fugitive cloud.   A cock cleared his throat in the

MR. GERHARDI AND NATURE.

yard below. The rich odour of mown grass and the rays on the ricks of straw bade one live. I blessed my fate, which did not require that I was to be hanged at dawn, that I had sufficient to eat, and could go home and sleep in clean sheets on a feather bed.

IV

I found Mrs. Stanley in a state of considerable agitation. The Prince had gone off his head again. It was perfectly awful ! He had threatened to shoot every man, woman and dog in the *pension*. The landlord's daughter, just as she stood in her nightgown, had run down to town to fetch the police, and the Princess had to be hidden in the landlady's clothes-cupboard. The Prince spied a young man in the yard and fired at him. Luckily just missed him, and the young man had to climb the waterpipe to save his life.

" Quite unhinged, apparently ? "

" Oh, quite. Still, I'm not surprised he sees red, the Princess having taken up with a young local painter called Bursch. Devilishly handsome boy, this painter, though no doubt a blackguard."

" But why a blackguard ? "

" He seems to me a little cheeky—cocksure. When we are nice to the lower classes we are so with an effort ; and they take it as their due. You know, I so want to be with her to prevent any sort of vice taking place between them. The peasants here won't stand for it. I'm sure the peasants in the village will rise. There's so much wickedness and

55

immorality in the world ! I feel sorry for Anton. He's such a boy. And *so* good-looking."

" But mad as a hatter."

" Oh, quite mad, of course."

" The clouds are dark, heavy." I looked at the mountains. " But it won't rain. They are no more than burden notes meant to show up the better the enchantment of the soaring and passionate summer day."

" I don't want to sleep, do you, after all these alarms and excursions ? I'm not a bit tired, really. I am—I will make a confession—I am fifty-seven. You'll tell no one ? "

" I only write."

" I have been away for years—and unhappy. Roaming, always roaming about. . . . I had a room where the rats jumped over my bed all the night ; and I, alone, abandoned in cold, unfriendly Peking. Perfectly awful."

" Peking ? Why did you go to Peking ? "

" To help the cause of Tsing-Lung. I wish I hadn't. The skunk, you know, turned out ungrateful and had nothing but abuse for me, for all I've done for him ! It was perfectly awful ! But I told him straight what I thought of him.

" You know, I think the yellow races are a real and awful menace and ought to be stamped out of the world. They're perfectly dreadful ! "

" Here, at any rate, you're safe and quiet."

" I want to go to Russia before I die. One doesn't live for ever, you know, and I so want to help the Bolsheviki."

" Oh, yes."

" I want to go and help Trotzki."

" I see."

" I don't believe in all these tales of atrocities. Capitalist fabrications, of course."

" Of course."

" Of course."

" Have you no people of your own ? "

" I loathed my family. My father was a perfect fool who used to go about asking every day of his life what the world was coming to, and who would clean our boots under Socialism : as if there weren't always people enough who were fit for nothing better. His one desire, having been born a gentleman, was to die one. And perhaps that was all he was fit for.

" My mother died of a bad temper. I *was* relieved ! She hated us and married us off, out of spite, to all the notorious imbeciles in the neighbourhood—thought it would serve us right. But I hated my husband. A fathead of a squire—you know the type. With no mind at all. In the morning he would go to inspect his pigs. And in the afternoon he would go to inspect his pigs. And in the evening he would go to inspect his pigs. And when visitors called on us he would hide himself behind a bush. He thought, the fool, that he had a position to keep up. But I told him he had none. He liked his land. But I said to him : ' I hate living in your pigsty.' "

" Where is he now ? "

" He's dead, the brute."

" You have no children, Mrs. Stanley ? "

" I have a daughter, a perfect she-ass—as dense as a cow."

" Where is she ? "

" She is married to a miserable little wretch of a man. But they are happy, the fools ! "

" Mrs. Stanley, you are—you are a bitter woman : you are an embittered woman."

" Am I bitter ? You know, I despise human nature ! "

" It dawns."

" Yes, gradually it dawns."

" I am Hamlet, you are Donna Quixote. I just want to wonder at this incredible wonder, our life, too beautiful to bear. You must needs do things, silly things, useless things ; still, you must do them."

" I must."

" You are sixty, I am twenty-seven. How much more have you to go ? But my life also will be over in a flash. What does life want ? from us ? from itself ? Does it know ? What is that grief, not ours, that you and I bear in our souls ? "

She sighed.

" In remote days this earth must have been organic —a huge animal, breathing and panting. These rocks are his bones, this earth the rotting flesh, this water the blood."

" And we, creeping insects fattening on his corpse."

" Oh, what clouds ! Blue, orange, dark violet, dark blue, still darker blue. A symphony in blue."

" Only like fountain-pen ink." She snorted. " You know, it gives one the blues ! "

" And a rent in the sky : the pure blue where dwell the angels."

" I don't want peace in the next world, do you ?
I want a little excitement."

" But not of the shooting kind."

" No. Good heavens, we haven't been to bed,
and now it is morning."

V

Morning. The Inn valley stretches deep beneath
us. More mountains, like ghost ships on an un-
charted sea, loom into sight as we climb the spiral
grass-edged path, meeting more flowers on our way :
snowdrops, buttercups, daisies, bluebells, primulas,
violets, while little brooks skurry down head-over-
heels to announce that spring is already come. An
hour's distance from our goal we spread out our
mantles on the green slope of a sheltered warm
valley, where daffodils grow in profusion by the
side of a brook, and stretch our limbs and doze
rapturously in the sun. Rising, we set out on the
last but one stage in our journey, climbing hills
without paths, cutting across pastures where frisky
young cows, turned irresponsible on these heights,
jump over the moon ; now clearing gurgling
brooks which still run hurry-skurry down to the
valleys to tell the glad tidings ; now stopping to
drink the cool water. By two we reach the top of
the shaggy mountain slope : above looms the gleaming naked dead rock of the summit. A separate
journey, after an hour's repose.

We lie on the edge of a plateau projecting
perilously over the void and look down at Inns-
bruck, miniature as on a map, the River Inn

bedded in the soft, green folds of the valley, the parcelled fields, the dotted villages, the spired churches, all lucent and serene in the spring sun. We climb the steep rocky way to the peak, clinging to loose stones and sending them rolling a mile or two till they rebound with a heavy earthen thud in the abyss. No more shrubs or alpine roses ; nor a human habitation anywhere. The last was the Gasthaus, which is now lost to sight. On we climb till, in the first dusk, we reach the flat rocky mountain top ; there is nowhere higher to go. The air is amazingly light. I sit on a rock, struck speechless by the mighty spectacle ; the neighbouring mountain peaks, all level now and grandly equal, look into the gathering dusk, heavy with unspoken utterance.

Mrs. Stanley looked on, wrapped in thought. " You know, I can't have this on my conscience. The Princess, I hear, is going off with the young painter Bursch on a honeymoon to Munich. What *will* the peasants think ! I'm sure I don't know. For the sake of sheer decency, I say, she could have waited a little. What was the hurry ? "

" There is nothing so urgent, so gripping, so pressing as love. Devilishly handsome woman ! "

" Alone with that young brute ! . . . After all my kindness . . . while I am to take her dog out for exercise. But when they return—the peasants here won't stand it. I'm sure the peasants in the village will rise. I really think it's my duty to go with them—to warn the hotel proprietors."

VI

From the balcony where I sit writing is the view of high mountains and below gurgles the angry turbulent Inn ; the sun blazes like fury, and tender birches and bristling firs reach up to my window. . . .

The postman comes up the hill. A letter from Mrs. Stanley. Lilac notepaper. Don't I know it ! I open it and read :

" She is wearing the Prince's mother's jewels, and Bursch the Prince's Russian riding-boots, and the peasants are bowing and kowtowing before them. But the more sensible ones have nicknamed him ' The Prince Bursch.' And she drinks like a fish and goes out with his pals—all local village lads—to the village pub and drinks beer with them, and they sing brawling songs and she joins in. And at the end they call on her to pay for it all and she opens her bag and pays. Perfectly awful ! Bursch has asked her to give him the money beforehand, to save appearances. But she is not the woman to part easily with her purse. She clings to two straws—her man and her pounds.

" That awful Swiss arrived here to-day and is on my heels all day long, but I avoid looking at him—so as not to be sick. I have danced with old Herr Bursch and the young scamp too—very good-looking but a bounder ; and the Princess looked jealous, I am bound to remark ! It was no proper dancing hall but a veritable dark hole we danced in, and Bursch stepped on my foot on purpose. The Princess chooses dark places like that on grounds of inherent immorality. I allowed myself that small

61

lapse for life is so dull. It poured all day long. Perfectly awful !

" Friday.—I follow them from town to town and warn all the hotels at which they have the temerity to put up of their not being married. Heaven knows I haven't many pounds to spare and this travelling after them is ruining me. And the hoteliers, I am sorry to say, are indifferent and unhelpful. One brute of a reception clerk, when I warned him that they weren't married, said, quite cynically : ' I do not care, madam.' I reported him on the spot to the manager who, I regret to say, is no better than he should be. I am told he goes round seducing all the maids in the hotel and even some of the visitors—it's perfectly awful—so I don't expect much help from him for fear of being bepawed by him myself. It would be so dreadful—though quite a handsome young brute. So I am going to see the proprietor about the impudent reception clerk and will not rest till he is dismissed. It's perfectly awful.

" Tuesday.—Seen the proprietor. An awful hound, no better than his menials. Told him what I thought of him. He will not do anything of his own accord, so went and informed the police of him—but so far without result. I will not rest even if I have to go to the Minister of Justice.

" Thursday.—The police seem to be hand in glove with the proprietor. This place is a nest of thieves. Vice, gross immorality everywhere, and corruption. One's soul literally sickens at the appalling dross and mud one meets in this connection ; all one's hopes of moral rectitude and virtue prove blind alleys ; the tremendous effort is productive of nothing but accumulated hatred, and one is choked out of one's senses by the muddy backwash of deceit, lies, sordid motives, and all the symptoms of lust, vice, and lewd debauchery. I visibly lose heart, fighting as I am here single-handed, and sometimes think life is a great disappointment.

" P.S.—Have heard the Princess prior to her marriage to the Prince was a circus woman in Dublin. Have put a detective to watch her.

" Sunday.—This morning went to the Princess to remonstrate with her—but hopeless. You know, I think the peasants in the village will do something. I want to shake you up to come here and work for the cause of public decency, surrounded by pitfalls and dangers of all kinds, and the labourer should lose no time in setting foot in the vanguard ! I hear the Princess wants to rent a villa. Went to warn the proprietor.

" Friday.—She's hired the villa, my protests notwithstanding, and already there are wrath and contention. They pretended their little maid Sophie had stolen socks and handkerchiefs and things. All a put-up affair, I'm convinced. The Princess drinks like a fish and—I shouldn't be at all surprised —has robbed herself in her less lucid hours. But they've turned poor Sophie out in what she stood in, all because she knew too much ! Poor little thing, I gave her tea in my room and she said they'd turned her out to make room for Bursch's mother, who now does all the cooking for them. And I hear old Bursch has given up his sausage shop and lives with them too. Perfectly awful !

" Monday.—Went and took a bath at the Princess's, as baths so expensive at hotel. Nasty-looking towel. I'm sure all the Bursch family use it in turn ; it looks as much : if they ever take a bath at all, which I doubt by the looks of them. But she is madly in love with young Bursch and all day long makes eyes at him, but Bursch, who is visibly getting tired of her, will only take her money, her good old English pounds, and serve her right ! The woman is a fool . . ."

VII

Another letter :

" It's perfectly awful. The Princess has chased out Bursch and has taken in a young Czech pianist, and has turned out all the Burschs, lock, stock and barrel. Poor people, they have nowhere to go ; they've sold the old cottage and spent all the money and now they are in the street. Old man Bursch came to me ; he cried in my room. I gave them lunch in my hotel. But heaven knows I have not many pounds to spare, and this is ruining me ! Young Bursch threatens to commit suicide and has shot twice at the pianist—but missed him, thank God."

VIII

Another letter :

" I warn you all against the wiles and cunning of that woman. Sophie was accused by her of stealing in order to make her out a common thief and a

WHEN THE PRINCESS TOOK UP WITH A CZECH PIANIST INSTEAD, THE
AUSTRIAN PAINTER SHOT TWICE AT HIM, BUT MISSED.

prison bird whose tongue should be valueless against her. Now isn't that mean? She took away from her all the pretty Tyrolese things she'd given her, and poor Sophie was sent home to her stepfather, in what she stood in, to mind the geese. For there is no end to that woman's iniquities. But she will rue it. Oh, she will have to pay for it! It's perfectly awful! She seduced an innocent young chemist, a nice hard-working modest young lad, a friend of Bursch, and she had them both arrested —because she'd had enough of both and wanted a change—on a false charge, I am convinced an entirely put-up affair, for both lads are as honest as day—arrested for leaving the hotel without paying their bill. The poor things—of course, they had no money, expecting her to pay for them since they were actually her guests. I was so sorry for them ; I used to send them food to the police station. But, you know, it never reached them ! The police is one mass of corruption. It's perfectly scandalous. And she has turned out the pianist, too, and has taken up with a Finn poet who dispenses altogether with words, expressing his sensibility entirely in logarithms, which, he says, conduces to an orgasm of emotional intensity unknown in language. Very strange. I thought it would interest you as a writer. But, oh, I hope the peasants will rise ! She wants to marry the Finn. I know, because she asked me : ' How is it in England, when a titled woman marries a commoner ? Is she allowed to retain her title ? ' I said : ' Only by courtesy ; and she wouldn't be much thought of if she did.' ' H'm,' she said. That was all. The man is as sensual as a tom cat.

E 2

It's perfectly awful ! Finns, I say, ought to remain in their own country. I hear they are well up in all sorts of vice. The woman's a second Catherine the Great. It's perfectly awful ! I did what I could to stop it. I went straight to the Mayor. But the idiot, you know, only shrugged his fat shoulders. ' Human nature,' he said lamely. Which is but another name for vice and indulgence. But Sophie prophesied a sad end for her. ' She will be robbed of all her possessions,' she said, ' just as she has robbed the young Prince of his own.' And I believe it : *I believe it !* "

IX

I did not stay long enough in the Tyrol to see Mrs. Stanley return from Munich. In her last letter to me when I was already in England she wrote : " I am through with Munich. I am going out to help the Riffs and the Bolsheviki. My friend Abd-el-Krim is hard pressed. . . . There is so much wickedness in the world, so much cruelty everywhere. . . ."

I revisited the Tyrol four years later. I wondered whether I would find Mrs. Stanley at the old *pension*. As dawn lifted the night and the sun smiled on the Tyrol snows, I ceased to think. Towards midday the train arrived at Kuffstein. The whole country was deep in snow and the sun shone over dell and hill benignantly. As there was no conveyance, I took the tram to the foot of the hill, and then set out quickly, girdling my way past the mountain villages. As I climbed up the hill, the snow-clad pines looked expectant and everything waited and

BUT HE ONLY SHRUGGED HIS SHOULDERS AND SAID "HUMAN NATURE . . . !"

watched. In the winter silence of frozen brooks, suddenly, as I listened, it seemed to me I had come near, quite near, the initial mystery of existence : that if somehow I could hold on for one more minute I should be touching the fringe of eternal being.

I was not wrong. Mrs. Stanley was at the *pension*. Six months ago she had quarrelled with the land-lady, but having no home of her own, had come back, she said, to die here. And, indeed, when I saw her that morning from my balcony dragging her poor bones up the hill, I thought to myself : she is not for long. Mrs. Stanley did not disguise her knowledge either.

" I know. They warned me at Casablanca, before I left Morocco, that it was hopeless my going. But I came. I was so frightened I might die there among the Riffs. Heat, dust, disease, base ingratitude everywhere. . . . Life is a great disappointment. . . . You know, when it comes to the end, one doesn't care."

I sighed and said nothing.

" My life's gone. How quickly it's gone. I haven't had time to turn round—and it's gone. To think that my clean body will decompose, begin to smell. . . . Ugh ! it's unbearable. I don't want to die ; for I have never lived. I have wasted my days so unprofitably. The proposals I've had in my time ! I turned a cold shoulder to every one ; a deaf ear to every entreaty. Was it spite ? Habit ? Bitterness ? It became a sort of second nature. Why ? I didn't want to be like that. But I was, despite myself somehow . . . and all the time, all the time I felt that it wasn't me, that *I* was being submerged, my real nature kept under. . . . I was beautiful. Who had not heard in my time of Mrs. Stanley, ' the beautiful Mrs. Stanley,' they used always to say. And the men ! The men ! And the Society papers ! . . . I never loved anyone. I was too cold, too selfish, too scornful, too fastidious, I suppose. No one was good enough. No one——"

" Oh, you're belying yourself ! "

" Only once—that was in India—I saw a man— and I quailed. But he arrived the week I was leaving Simla. My passage was booked. What could I do ? "

" Was he an . . . an Indian ? "

" He was a colonel . . . on the General Staff. We were friends, the only eligible people in the hotel. He knew I was afraid of mice, and I used to ask him to see me upstairs to my room. And once . . ."

" Once——? "

" Once he wished to stay. It was the night before I sailed. He pleaded. But I wouldn't listen. My passage was booked. What could I do ?

" I have made a mess of my life."

" We all do."

" No, no ! I should have listened to him and stayed on. I should have followed him to the ends of the earth. But I took the boat and went home.

" You know, I believe there's something strange and uncanny about this life in the flesh, as if we'd strayed into the wrong place, a region not meant for us."

" Where angels fear to tread. But we hardened beasts ruminate in abject, if bewildered, resignation, dimly conscious of a nobler heritage."

" Just so. When I was born, they tell me I laughed all day long to myself. My soul was a bright star. Gradually it lost its brightness, as if—uncanny thought !—they'd shut it up in a cold damp cellar. And so I couldn't see. My lamp had grown quite dim.

" But I am not frightened of the coming of night, for in pitch dark it will shine brighter than ever."

" Brave words these."

" It isn't me——"

" Isn't me——? "

" —that dies. It's what you've conjured up of me in your own mind."

" A phantom—like a Frenchman's notion of an Englishman."

" Fit to perish. Like this poor flesh. But I, scenting pollution, will sniff at it and go home."

I remember that afternoon. It was the first day of the Carnival. In the yard below a violinist had begun to play an air from the " Gräfin Maritza," and they were dancing.

Almost the last words I can recall of our discourse that evening were : " I wouldn't stop in Russia. That home of disappointment. . . . My help was scorned."

" Yes ? "

" Trotzki has turned out ungrateful. Abd-el-Krim refused me a pass for the war zone. Base ingratitude everywhere. There is so much wickedness in the world . . . *so* much wickedness . . . ! "

73

" What is one against a host ? "

" All one has done seems so . . . so finical, so unimportant now. You know, I am so . . . lonely. All my life I've been lonely. And all I have done I have done because I was lonely."

" Yes, yes."

" I wanted to do good."

" Of course."

" People are so wicked, the most appalling——"

" Yes."

X

I visited Kuffstein again the following winter. I took the little mountain railway to the *pension*. It wound and wound, girdling the snow-covered hills in a spiral. It was now quite dark. I got out at the little station, and shuffled through the dark forest on my way to the *pension*. There was a full moon as I crossed the forest. The pines laden with snow and swaying in the wind seemed to be telling each other something. For a moment I looked at them and wondered.

At the *pension* I learnt Mrs. Stanley had died a month previously and was buried in the village churchyard lower down on the hill.

I opened my windows. How fresh the morning air was ! How quiet the mountains. One forgot the great height one was on because here the mountain peaks were all level, and they were silent.

They were silent ! With the great, cavernous silence of things. Here was peace, uttered long before us ! The mountain peaks, all on a level, were listening, straining over, pricking their ears. On these heights they communed. Hush ! Could you hear ?—" We shan't say anything . . . shan't say anything. . . ."

The First Time I had an " Affaire "

by

BEVERLEY NICHOLS

HER name was Pearl. Pearl what, I neither know nor care. I like to think of her as Pearl, and nothing else, a rounded, glistening entity, detached from the family shell.

Rounded, she certainly was, at the age of seven, and glistening too, after she had been dancing in a hot room. And it was thus that I first met her, at the dancing class of Madame Muller, in a seaside town on the south coast of England, which I adorned when I was eight years old.

And yet, I believe, no brass plates have been attached to the walls of Madame Muller's establishment, to indicate the precise spot where my first love burgeoned. It is to be hoped (and believed), that after this article, at least one impressive plaque will be subscribed by the Mayor and Corporation.

The dancing class was held on Tuesdays and Fridays, from four till six. One walked up a long drive bordered with chestnut trees, to a Victorian house, clutching a brown paper parcel. This parcel, when undone, revealed a pair of " Court " shoes and a pair of white kid gloves. One wore an Eton suit.

I shall never forget the day when I first met Pearl, because my mother had provided me, by some mischance, with two right-hand gloves. This

79

seemed, at the time, a crisis of the first order. What could one possibly do? I stood in the corner of the room, vainly trying to pull one of the gloves over my left hand, but the thumb stuck out and the thing looked wrinkled and ridiculous. Bravely I decided to face the music. I walked across the shiny floor . . . (how empty and desert-like it seemed, with all the little girls in their pale pinks and blues staring at one!) . . . and I whispered to Madame Muller the hideous truth.

Instantly, that resourceful woman produced the solution. " Wear one, and carry the other ! " she cried. Before I could express my appreciation of this brilliant idea, she had forgotten me, and was clapping her hands for silence. And as I hurried back to the wall, I heard her voice ring out . . .

" Pearl, darling ! Your solo, please."

II

From the row of pale pinks and blues stepped a little girl in white. She was plump, and dark, with large brown eyes. Her hair was very smooth and shiny, and she had a white bow over each of her ears. But it is possible that these allurements might not have sufficed to complete my downfall had it not been for her astonishing self-possession. I have never seen anybody so completely sure of herself. A prima ballerina, surrounded by bounding débutantes at a charity matinée, could not have been more supremely confident.

And then, she began to dance.

The dance, as these jaded eyes recall it, was on the naïve side. It was a Symbolic Dance, and as we all know, when you are doing a Symbolic Dance the great thing is to look as if you had lost something. Pearl was grand at this. She not only looked as if she had lost something, but the whole of the dance was nothing more than an elaborate tripping after this something. As soon as the first chord was struck on the bronchial piano she drew her little plump form up to its full height of four feet, curved her hand with a dramatic gesture over her eyes, as though shielding them from the sun, and craned her neck slowly and rhythmically round the room. The parents upon whom her stare fastened felt quite hot, and shuffled their feet, or averted their eyes. But Pearl was unconscious of them. She was too busy being Symbolical. And as the dance went on, and she pirouetted round the room, continuing her eager search, bending one knee to the floor and staring up to the sky, turning swiftly round and scanning the walls, I became more and more enraptured. At last, thank heavens, she found It, whatever It may have been, and she tossed this imaginary It up in the air, skipping and laughing, over and over again, in a triumphant canter round the room. And by a happy chance, the music stopped just as she was opposite me.

III

How I summoned up the courage to ask her to dance I do not know. But I did. And I was accepted. Yes . . . in a moment we were bouncing round the room to the music of a Highland Schottische.

" It was lovely," I said breathlessly, " your dance."

" Thank-you," replied Pearl.

" Are you going on the stage ? " I asked.

" I expect I shall," she volunteered. " But don't tell mother, please."

I vowed that nothing would induce me to tell her mother. I felt as though this vow constituted some sort of bond between us. Whether Pearl felt the same, I do not know, for she was inclined to be taciturn. The only subject on which she was at all voluble was the jealousy of the other little girls.

" They all think I'm stuck up," she said, " just because Madame Muller asks me to do the solos."

" It's jealousy," I breathed fervently.

Pearl nodded. " That's what mother says," she observed. And then, with the true passion of the artist, she became absorbed once more in the dance. " One two *three* four, one two *three* four," she chanted, as we hopped round the room.

This was the first of many dances.

By the time the first daffodils were out under the chestnuts in the drive, I was deeply in love.

IV

There were only two other little boys in the class. One was very plain, and covered with spots, so he is best forgotten. The other was very good looking. He was also a Prince, so we may remember him. Prince Victor de Polignac was his name. He was a charming companion, whose only drawback was his passion for collecting dead mice and keeping them till they became skeletons. To this end, he founded a club, of which I was Honourable Treasurer, called

" The Skelly Club." *Malheureusement* . . . the few deceased objects of the animal kingdom which came our way . . . such as thrushes, mice, and one rat, obstinately refused to become skellies. They appeared to have no right ideas about the proper principles of decomposition.

It was Pearl's antipathy to " The Skelly Club " which caused the first crisis in my life.

" I think it's horrid," she said one day, " all those skellies. Besides . . ." she added, somewhat illogically, " you haven't got any decent ones."

" We *shall* have," I protested eagerly. " By the summer we shall have heaps."

She paused, as though pondering whether it would be worth her while to wait till the summer, in order to share our morbid pleasures. She decided it was not worth while. She wrinkled her nose again and said : " I think it's horrid. If you liked *me*, you wouldn't do that sort of thing."

And she turned away, and stalked haughtily across the room.

This was agony. The rest of the dancing-class was unutterably bitter. When it was over I tried to catch her, to ask her if she really meant what she said, but she eluded me. And so, with a heavy heart, I decided that I must do the manly thing, and put skeletons out of my life for ever.

I announced my decision to Prince Victor de Polignac as we were changing our shoes in the hall. The following dialogue took place :—

Myself. I say, Polly, I'm going to resign from the club.

Prince. What ? Why ?

Myself (faintly). I think it's rather a stinking club, anyway.

Prince. It isn't stinking. You haven't given it a chance.

Myself. Yes I have. And, anyway, nothing ever happens. Nobody ever finds anything.

Prince. We shall. (Darkly.) There are rats in our house. And I've got some poison.

Myself (weakening). I bet they don't eat it. And even if they do, you won't get them. They'll go off and moulder away somewhere.

Prince. Oh no, they *won't*. It's a special sort of poison.

What would have happened at that moment, had not Pearl swept into view, I do not know. It is quite possible that I might have succumbed to the lures of the chase, that my whole life might have been different, that I might at this moment, be shouldering a rifle instead of clutching a pen . . . pouring lead into quantities of large and amiable animals in darkest Africa.

However, Pearl passed by. Her plump little face was highly lifted. She ignored me. It was more than I could bear. The dialogue came to an abrupt end . . .

Myself. Anyway, I'm resigning.

Prince (contemptuously). You're a sissy if you do.

Myself. So are you, whether you do or not. And you stink.

Thus ended a Great Friendship.

If Mr. Nichols hadn't Left The Skelly Club . . .?

V

After that, things went fairly smoothly. My mother called on hers, and the call was returned. Oh—those Edwardian calls ! Tea was laid in the brown drawing-room at half-past three, and from half-past three till four my mother sat, staring at a fantastically elaborate collection of cakes and sandwiches. Then there was the sound of the cab on the gravel drive, and my mother rang the bell before the caller had alighted from the cab, in order that the parlour-maid might be crouching in the appropriate position behind the front door, to wrench it open as soon as the caller *had* alighted.

And then, small-talk, and " would you like to see the garden ? " And Pearl and I would escape to another room, which contained my favourite piano, and I would play and she would dance. Beachcomber, the savage clown of the *Daily Express*, who interests me more as a social phenomenon than as an individual intelligence, would have been physically sick at the sight of us. I desire no more gracious compliment.

There were letters, of course. Letters were much more exciting in those days. You began by ruling lines across the notepaper, very faintly, in pencil. Then you deposited a certain amount of youthful spittle on the nib, because you had to have a new nib, and unless you spat on the nib before dipping it in the ink, nothing happened. Even after you *had* spat, nothing very much happened. Only this sort of thing :—

Dear Pearl,

I am having a party on Wednesday, April the second, and shall be very pleased if you will come. Please stay late, if you come, till seven. I have an electric light set over my bed, it is very nice, and the bateries are under the bed.

Yours affectionately,

Beverley Nichols.

To which, the response, on pink paper, with a capital P in gold at the top . . . (there was grandeur for you !) . . . was as follows :—

Dear Beverley,

I shall be very pleased to come to your party on Wednesday, April the second. Mother says I can stay till half past six. I will come in a cab and bring my dancing-shoes. I will be very pleased to look at the bateries. I have had three new kittens but Mother says two will have to be drowned.

Yours affectionately,

Pearl.

What mystery ! What allure ! What sophistication ! I cannot go on writing " What," but you see what I mean ? Pearl . . . in a cab. Crunching down the drive. While I pressed my nose against the window pane, and darted out to greet her before the housemaid could intervene. Pearl . . . with her dancing-shoes, which were gravely unwrapped, and laid on the old oak chest which stood in the darkness of the hall. Pearl, looking at the " bateries." . . .

VI

It was all so swift, so bitterly transient. A few dances, a few letters, a few parties, and it was finished, in a way which I am about to describe.

But it did not *seem* swift, then. Time, when one was very young, was marked " Lento, andante cantabile." The clock in the nursery and the clock in the library had different measures.

Nor was it only Time that was different, in Youth. The lilacs were lovelier, and the song of the blackbird more liquid. The twilights of April were longer, and the thrushes that hopped across the lawns were as large as hens. Cats scratched more fiercely and purred with a superior appeal. Men were taller (and far, far wiser), women were more rounded and smelt nicer. (If that sounds faintly disgusting it is your mind, not mine. I was thinking of a scent that is still very sweet to me . . . the scent of a violet powder that my mother used to use. It was kept in a charming little silver box, and sometimes I used to go into her bedroom and dab a wallop of it on the end of my nose, and gaze, fascinated, at the grotesque reflection. Provincial papers please copy.)

Of course, there is no story in this story. No climax. You cannot end something which you have not begun.

All that happened was that one day, Pearl and her mother came to tea. After tea, when we had played the piano and looked at the " bateries," we went into the garden. We walked down a winding path. And suddenly Pearl turned to me and said :

" We're leaving."

" You . . . you're leaving ? "

" We're going to live in London."

" Pearl ! "

The world was very still, just then. I took her hand in mine. Our fingers were very sticky. We had been eating toffee.

" My father's lost his money," she said gravely.

" Oh, Pearl ! "

More and more silent became the world. It was as though someone had set his fingers to the earth's lips, and hushed every bird that sang.

And then she began to cry. Very silently, in a strangely grown-up way. Big tears rolled down her pale cheeks. But she did not utter a sound.

" Don't go," I said.

She shook her head.

" Don't go, Pearl," I said again. " I love you."

And there we kissed. Under the immense, blossoming chestnut tree, whose white candles were being lit by the lazy dusk. Two small bodies pressed together, awkwardly, absurdly . . . for a curious, dim moment of Youth, in which many things were foreshadowed. Of course, it is always the things which come after which make the things which are . . . it is always the last act which gives beauty and significance to the first, just as the line of Death is always the only line which could possibly be drawn to give " composition " to the medley of life. And so, perhaps, under the chestnut tree, there fluttered over both of us the dark and restless wings of unborn loves, and in the rustling of the

leaves there came the echo of many distant adora‑
tions. I do not know. I only know that for a
moment we were lovers.

And then Pearl sniffed, and said : " You bumped
my nose."

The First Time I Really Travelled

by
BETTY ASKWITH

HAVE you ever applied "Samuel Butler's test"? This is not so formidable as it sounds, it does not involve the use of a laboratory and litmus paper—but it is a very searching one all the same. For Samuel Erehwon-not-Hudibras Butler once said that one was only really enjoying oneself when one was not looking forward, however faintly or secretly at the very bottom of one's heart, to the time when the experience would come to an end. Try it next time you are at a party or at the Queen's Hall or on a water chute.

My great-uncle, Sir Roger Palmer, was a man who, I imagine, would have had very little in common with Samuel Butler. Nevertheless, one day riding home from hunting, he asked himself, "Do I really enjoy this?" and he answered himself, "No." So when he got home he sold all his horses and he never hunted again. One always imagines that that ride home must have been very unpleasant, that they had had a bad day, that he was wet and starting a cold, that his horse wouldn't walk properly and would only jiggle, and that he had refused an easy place under the eyes of the entire field. We all know those moments, mentally I had always blamed Uncle Roger for precipitancy and pig-headedness.

95

And yet I don't know—the time that I applied Samuel Butler's test to travelling was as fair a moment to choose as might be. It was about midnight and we were between Salzburg and Prague. We had no sleeper. A man opposite us was extended on the other seat and we were sharing one, head to feet. I was travelling with Theodora Benson, the editor of this book, who, in addition to her other perfections as a travelling companion, and they are many, is very, very slender. But however slender your companion, two on a railway carriage seat is one too many. We had no pillows and I could feel the scratchy plush of the second-class compartment underneath my cheek. The arm I was lying on was beginning to get cramp and I was wedged between Theodora and the back of the seat so that moving was impossible without a terrific disturbance. In about half an hour we were due at the frontier where there would be passports and customs. We had an hour to wait in Prague from 6 to 7 a.m. We had been travelling more or less uncomfortably for two months. But when I applied S. B.'s test to travelling it came out triumphantly. I didn't even much want this particular journey to end ; I suppose if an angel had flown down and told me it would continue to infinity I should have complained a bit, but as it was I was quite happy. And when I thought that a week from that day we should be in our comfortable homes, sleeping on really soft beds every night, with delicious regular meals and baths whenever we wanted them, I could have wept with sorrow. I had been bitten with the travel bug.

And for the first time. I had never really travelled before. I had " been abroad " heaps of times. I had been to the Italian lakes, to Palestine, to South America, but I had never travelled. It is not a question of distance. One could, I imagine, travel in England, one can, I am certain, go to China and back and not travel at all. What is travelling? It is difficult to say. I know what it is not. It is not getting from place to place on expensive and smooth-running boats and trains, it is not staying at the best European hotels or at the Legation and meeting charming people to whom you are introduced and whom you might very well know in London, it is not good games of tennis or bathing or watching the polo. All these things are extremely pleasant, but they are not travelling. In these surroundings one carries one's own atmosphere with one, one thinks, one remembers, one looks forward, one is a sentient and reasonable human being. When one travels one does and is none of these things, one's mind moves entirely in the present, never going beyond the thought of one's next meal, one doesn't try to fit things into one's life or into any kind of scheme, one just accepts them placidly, as they are, enjoying with an equal pleasure food, drink, scenery, and chance encounters with preposterous strangers. One also accepts placidly, as they are, sleeping in trains, no baths, indifferent sanitary accommodation, getting up and going to bed at odd times and meals of bread and chocolate. My stomach on one occasion did, I must say, refuse to accept placidly a meal of not very fresh red caviare, eaten on sweet Marie biscuits because we

had no bread (the biscuits were in addition slightly
flavoured with cloves, because the mosquito bite
stuff had broken in the suitcase and permeated
everything), chocolate and sweet red wine which
had got very hot and rather mulled in the sun. In
fact it rebelled passionately, but this was the only
time it or we minded anything at all.

To describe the whole of that journey the first
time I travelled would go far beyond the limits of
this book, it would also encroach seriously on the
very brilliant and witty book (Advt. and I ought to
get at least another guinea for it), which is going to
be written by Miss Benson, on that subject. But a
little cross section of it, three days between Salonika
and Skoplje, will, I think, show what I mean. There
were no excitements, we met no brigands, saw
nothing of I.M.R.O., that sinister organisation,
did, felt and saw nothing that was " news," and
yet, in however mild and dull a fashion, we were, I
think, really travelling.

The train drew into Bitolj about half-past three
in the afternoon. We were glad to be in Jugo-
Slavia. It was for the most mundane of reasons,
we had run out of Greek drachmæ. After intensive
search in every pocket we possessed, we had at
last found one, value—½d. This enabled us to buy
a twist of bread faintly speckled with caraway seeds
at a wayside station. We ate it with chocolate,
this was our lunch, breakfast had been at 6.30 a.m.
that morning. Now we were in Jugo-Slavia, and
as rich as lords, possessing over £6. (The tragic
thing was that in Würzburg several weeks later,
when we had run out of German money and were

prowling round a sausage-stall, positively aching for forty pfennigs, I found a *cache* of no less than *fifteen* drachmæ.)

It had, except for the lack of food, been a pleasant journey from Salonika. We had talked with a Greek business man and engineer, who had been draining the land about there. He told us a lot of interesting facts about Greece, the peasants, the economic situation, the refugees ; he also told us many stories about his English colleagues. They were bad stories, sometimes incomprehensible, with very little point, but through them all one got a fascinatingly clear picture of " young Ferris." Smaller public school and university. Very young and immature, absolutely straight, sometimes high-spirited but morose in the mornings, longing to go on leave, amazingly limited and somehow lovable. Asking his colleagues and subordinates in the office in for a cup of tea, and annoyed and impatient because they didn't go after half an hour, whereas the Greeks in the sociable Continental fashion intended to sit and talk for the rest of the afternoon. Asking our friend point blank how much commission he was getting on a horse he was advising " young Ferris " to buy, which scandalised him very much though he was tolerant of such queer manners—yet lending another Greek £5 on an I.O.U. and being immensely surprised when the Greek refused to acknowledge it. Refraining his eyes scrupulously from the Greek girls because his mother had warned him that if he got " mixed up " with them he would, inevitably, be shot.

Our nice Greek friend with his thin intelligent

G 2

face left us before the frontier. He told us a lot about Greek politics which I have unhappily forgotten, though I do remember that he was strongly against the possibility of a restoration, not from any anti-monarchist sentiment, but because he believed that few Greeks cared a damn one way or the other.

He was replaced, and not to our advantage, by the Customs officials. They were fat and sleepy, and though they showed no animosity of any kind, they insisted on our opening every piece of our luggage, and there was a lot of it, and it was heavy. They didn't help us get it down off the rack either. I don't know what they would have done if they'd found anything. One of them pointed to a box of Turkish delight in my bag and asked, " *Qu'est que c'est que ca ?* "

" *Des bonbons,*" I replied.

" *Des bombes ?* " he queried in a perfectly routine tone, rather the tone of one who wanted to get the thing clear, but wasn't going to take any action about it. Perhaps he thought it all right if I was going to let them off in Jugo-Slavia.

The Jugo-Slav Customs didn't bother about " bombes." They searched several people on the train, but they waved us through with *empressement.* We waited a little on a little country platform in the sun, watching the Jugo-Slav military guard showing the Greek military guard a turkey's egg, which had just been laid ; then we bundled into a very small rather sweet train, third-class passengers only, and in twenty minutes we were in Bitolj.

We scanned the platform with great interest, because we had been given an introduction to an

Betty Askwith

Archimandrite of the Greek Church by a Russian friend of ours, and we were naturally excited. We did not dare hope too much, but when we saw that tall black figure on the platform, we knew our utmost expectations were fulfilled.

I wish I could describe Archimandrite Constantine adequately. He wore, of course, the long black gown and black cylindrical cap of the Greek priest. His uncut hair was scraped into rather an untidy bun. His face was thin and ascetic with a high arched nose, very bright blue eyes and a fair brown beard. It was a face as I like to imagine the face of Christ. He was childlike in some ways, not in the least childish, but possessing that eager interest in present things, that open candour, which are the most pleasing characteristics of the Age of Innocence, and which for some reason are only found later in monks and nuns. It is not unselfishness, for children are certainly selfish, but it is perhaps a lack of self-interest. We met Father Constantine only once. We spent perhaps four hours in his company. We didn't speak on very intimate subjects, and yet we felt him, no, we knew him, to be that rare and felicitous combination, a saint, a scholar and a gentleman.

He brought with him, to meet us, a companion. A small dark very young-looking man, whom I took at first to be his son, not being versed in the various degrees of celibacy in the Orthodox Church, but who turned out to be a co-professor at the College. He seemed to be indispensable. He could only talk German which we have but smatterings of, and he took but a tepid interest in us. But he made a fourth wherever we went. Could it be he was necessary as a chaperone?

We drove to our hotel in a little horse carriage, and we were very gay and happy as we looked at Bitolj, with its ramshackle mixture of old and new, square white barracks and tumble-down Oriental houses, its churches and its minarets.

After we'd left our luggage and had a glass of tea, Archimandrite Constantine took us to see his church, San Demetro, which was beautiful. It was built in 1820, and in those days the Turks, being in possession, ordered for no particular reason that if it was to be built at all, it must be built within a month. So it was—and a good month's work it is.

Then we walked out through the town to see the excavations of the old Roman city of Heracleum. There is nothing much to see, the outline of an altar, a broken column or two, but the walk was very pleasant. The evening sunlight streamed over the snow-topped mountain and the vivid green of the meadows. We passed a couple of cemeteries, one Mohammedan, one Christian. We, or rather Father Constantine, were capped by groups of black-trousered theological students. We passed a sentry-box outside the Customs House, the interior of which was all decorated with lilac.

I walked with the other professor, who conversed in rapid and fluent German. Sometimes I understood, sometimes I didn't, it didn't seem to matter much in any case. At one point he broke off, and pointing to a mare and her foal, in a field, asked: " *Wie heisst es in Englisch?* "

"Horse," I replied, inaccurately but simply. I have never understood why this discouraged him so about the whole English language. He shook his head sadly, clicked his tongue once or twice and remained silent for quite ten seconds.

The excavations as I have mentioned are not yet much to see, but one thrilling and romantic thing there was. "Here," said Father Constantine, pointing to the little stream, "was the Roman bridge." One could just see the remains of it. A stone or two built into the bank. This was where the Roman road passed that ran through Ohrid and Heracleum to Salonika. Here had crossed the legions with eagles before them ; for a moment one could almost see the glint of sunshine on golden helmets, hear the steady tramp of marching feet. There is romance in roads and ports that no city can ever equal.

On the way back I walked with Archimandrite Constantine. This was very decent of Theodora because her German is even worse than mine. We did not talk of anything very special ; he told me about an ammunition explosion there had been at Bitolj just after the war. We discussed the assassination of King Alexander a little. He asked about our travels and when I told him we had been to Greece, he said : "*Ah le grec ancien—c'est mon passion !*" This was the most personal remark he made, and yet one had the feeling of something extraordinarily pleasant, of something spacious and noble in this desultory converse, as if the seeds of a friendship were being sown.

When we got back to the town, we went to see the

Theological College, of which he was head. I have a morbid interest in institution life, schools and barracks and prisons. It is perhaps because I hate them so much. It is at least a salutary tonic in one way. When inclined to grumble at my lot I can thank God that I am not a pupil in the Theological Seminary at Bitolj. Even being under Father Constantine would not reconcile me to those large spotlessly clean dormitories, those fifteen or sixteen little white beds, and no chair, no table, no curtains, to break the monotony, no sign of any kind of personal possession.

The Archimandrite's own room is small and bare enough. We studied his books, all theological, and then he very charmingly presented us with a copy each of a book written by himself, unfortunately in Russian. We asked him to write an inscription. What should he put? Well, that he must decide on for himself. He thought for some time and then said rather slowly, would it be quite all right if he put : "With best wishes." No, but really, was that as it should be, would I be sure to tell him if it wasn't? When Theodora's turn came he was quite ambitious and wanted to put something different. After some thought he hit on : "With kind regards." Was that all right? Were we quite sure it was absolutely proper and *convenable?*

In the evening light we strolled back to our hotel, the Archimandrite and, of course, the German Professor accompanying us. And it is now that I have my most vivid memory of Father Constantine. A small, very dirty child cannoned straight into him. He bent down, and murmuring some term of endearment and amusement, set it straight on its toddling course again. It was the most ordinary of actions, nearly any man we knew would have done the same, and yet the beauty and tenderness of that gesture are unforgettable.

I wish I could remember what we had for dinner. Except that halfpenny roll and a glass of tea on arrival, we hadn't eaten all day, so it was probably something pretty stupendous, but somehow it escapes my memory. All I know is that when it was over Theodora expressed a desire for yoghourt or sour cream, and we strolled down-town to find some.

On our way we found some very revolting post-cards in shiny glaze, of young men with quiffs and young women with pompadours and rolling eyes ; and we selected one of a young couple kissing the toes of a very fat baby, to send to Evelyn Waugh. This was in return for a well-chosen post-card of a basket containing three kittens which he had sent Theodora from Rome. She had written asking him about the essay now appearing in this book, and his post-card bore the simple legend : " Don't pester me."

The yoghourt shop doled us out the most enormous portion for two dinars or 4d. Luckily they also provided a family of five kittens, and here is an interesting example of the Mendelian theory. Four of those kittens and their mother lapped up the yoghourt with loud purrs, but the fifth refused to have anything to do with it. Or perhaps it just had a bilious attack.

After we had fed ourselves and the kittens to

bursting point, we strolled back along the main street and dropped into the cinema which conveniently was part of our hotel, and there, to our great joy, flickering and rather blotchy, but quite unmistakable, we saw the King greeting the Duke of Gloucester on his return from Australia. We had about ten minutes of the Wild West comic film that followed the news reel and then we went to bed.

Archimandrite Constantine and the German Professor came to see us off the next morning. The latter had lost all interest in us and was almost quite silent, but Father Constantine brought us the most enchanting presents of balls of wax twisted like string and adorned with little coloured designs, to burn in the churches. He also gave us a list of what we should see in Ohrid.

Then we piled ourselves and the luggage on to the motor 'bus, one of those useful one-storey Jugo-Slav vehicles, for which no road is too precipitous, no load too great, and waved good-bye to Bitolj and the tall black figure standing on the pavement.

We arrived at Ohrid about one o'clock, and straight away we hired a car to take us to the monastery of Sveti Naom which is the other side of the lake. Ohrid is, I think, the most lovely place that we struck on the whole of our trip, but one would have to be a Wordsworth to get away with a description of it. I will merely say that it is a lot of mountains, the lower slopes of which are cultivated and green and the upper slopes of which are not, stuck around an oblong shaped lake, with

the tiny town of Ohrid at one end and the monastery
of Sveti Naom at the other.

We spent a pleasant afternoon at Sveti Naom.
The order in which we did things is rather blurred in
my mind because we did most of them twice, once
poking round by ourselves and once shown round
by the monks. There were three of these. One, a
full-fledged father, with a thin ascetic face, a great
bushy black beard, and bright dark eyes. He
spoke no language but Serbo-Croat. One was a
novice, a great burly man who had been a sailor.
He wore, rather incongruously, grey flannel trousers
and tennis shoes under his robe and spoke fluent
but guttural French. The third monk was alleged
to speak every known language but was too shy to
utter a word in any. He was a moon-faced boy,
his round youthful chin uncomfortably adorned
with a very sparse unconvincing-looking fringe and
his uncut back hair sticking straight out like a
draggled drake's tail. Once he picked a spray of
lilac which we hoped was intended for us. We
looked at him encouragingly, rather hoping for it,
because we approved of the pleasant Balkan habit
of casually pressing flowers on one wherever one
goes. But his shyness was too much for him, we
never got that lilac.

In the middle of the courtyard round which the
monastery is built, is the original tenth-century
church. It is like all Byzantine churches of that
date and the best adjective I can find to describe it is
" cosy." It is golden brown in colour, small and
square with an octagonal tower crowned by a
round roof. Inside it is crowded and dark and full

of the peculiar charm of Orthodox Churches. I think I will never love any churches so much as these. They are never cold and bare with the curious earthy smell of Protestant churches or tawdry and cheap-looking like some Roman Catholic ones. A few candles prick the gloom with their golden points of light, the little oil lamps burn dimly before the icons. Sometimes these icons are old and mysterious, wonderfully painted, magnificently jewelled, sometimes they are quite humble and cheap ; sometimes there are faded frescoes and rather battered mosaics of incredible beauty and naïveté on the walls, sometimes they are simply washed with distemper ; but nevertheless in all these churches there is an atmosphere that eludes description. It does not give one a particularly *exalté* feeling. One strolls in, lights one's candle before the altar, moves about looking at things with one's hands in one's pockets. One can, one feels, move around, talk, eat sweets if one wishes, without irreverence or bravado—and yet one is unmistakably in the House of God. It is simple and natural, soothing and friendly. There is a warm present sense of spiritual comfort. One has come home.

There are, of course, exceptions to every rule, and I am going to make one right away. That is the new church at Sveti Naom. It is a sort of combined chapel and campanile, and it is built by a large sum of money given by " *le feu roi Alexandre.*" I am sure *le feu roi Alexandre* meant well, and I hope he is reaping his reward in heaven, but his action was, to say the least of it, ill-judged. Outside

The building is hideous, inside it is revolting. It is decorated with enormous over life-size frescoes. There is a Christ about 30 feet long, with a perfectly expressionless face like a silly sheep. He is surrounded by heads of angels, such angels! They are positively frightening. I feel sure whoever painted them must have had some sort of a Freudian complex. They have very long eyelashes and they leer at one out of the corners of their eyes in a positively lewd manner. They might have come straight out of a café chantant in Port Said. The only pleasing picture was one of a lion. He was St. Mark's lion, and he was reading over St. Mark's shoulder and he was plainly upset by what he read. His pleasant anxious face was all puckered, his eyes were round and his eyebrows climbed up to the roots of his mane in horrified amazement.

We were relieved from having to say much about the beauties of the chapel, by the constant interruptions of the goat. She was a white goat who had arrived on that morning as a present to the monastery, but she was not at all shy. She was a friendly creature, and whenever she saw two or three gathered together, she bounded up to make one of them. She also developed a great affection for the leather tassels that tied up my brogues. She found them very tasty. Repulses meant nothing to her. Twice she was turned out of the chapel, but when we entered the refectory she was still with us. Then someone took a firm line and shoved her out of the door and locked it on her. There were sounds of butting and kicking and then silence. Then through the door on the other side of the refectory

entered that goat. She came as if she had been
shot from a catapult, flouncing across the floor, her
hind quarters wriggling, her tail agitating madly,
drumming with her hooves. Never have I seen a
member of the brute creation express indignation
and resentment so clearly. She joined the group
around the table and settled down to eat the tassels
on my shoes.

I hope she found them as good as we found our
lunch. There were two kinds of fish, done very
tastily with rice and chopped herbs, and a big
bowl of butter beans, and red wine, and coffee and
rakija, which is a Jugo-Slav liqueur, which does
not taste of aniseed like the Turkish rakija does.
In my early novels, I mean the ones written between
the ages of seven and twelve, I was fond of describing
meals. " Thereupon they fell to, heartily," was
my usual method of concluding the description.
On this occasion we had had breakfast at seven,
and it was now three o'clock and the description is
a very apt one.

After lunch we met " *le fou*." He had had shell-
shock during the war and now he worked at the
monastery. He was quite harmless, the monk
explained, and answered sensibly when you spoke
to him, but unless questioned he never spoke. He
never asked for anything or originated anything or
greeted anyone. They wanted us to ask him questions in English because he had worked in America.
We asked him such trivial questions as when he had
gone there, what he had done. He answered as
they said quite sensibly, in English, but in a totally
expressionless voice. Then I asked him if he had

My girl-friend & I had a
difference of opinion by
Lake Ohrida.

MY GIRL-FRIEND AND I HAD A DIFFERENCE OF OPINION BY
LAKE OHRIDA.

[illegible] and his eyes were the most beautiful I have ever seen. They were big and brown, and they had the same beauty, the same dumb uncomprehending, unconsciously reproachful look that one sees in the eyes of a dying stag. There are no words to describe this tragedy, it was not horrible or frightening in the very least, but it seemed the saddest thing in the whole world.

It was coming back from Sveti Naom that we had the Great Quarrel. We had travelled together for over six weeks and no breeze had ruffled the serenity of our intercourse. We had survived discomfort, colds, bilious attacks, incompctence on the other one's part, sharing admirers, occasions when the admirers preferred Theodora, with an unshaken good temper and understanding. But this was a question different from these, it was an impersonal question, a question of abstract fact, of Right and Wrong. It ranked with the Problems of Transubstantiation, and whether seven angels can sit on a pin's head, and as everyone knows, these are the most impossible questions to settle without shedding of blood.

Now it happened that we had altered our watches by an hour (I cannot now remember which way) on leaving Greece for Jugo-Slavia. And one of us said as we drove away from Sveti Naom : " I think we shall have plenty of time to see the churches in Ohrid before it gets dark." And the other replied : " Yes, especially as we have an hour extra daylight." " No," said the first speaker, " we have an hour less." And on that we were off.

Theodora told me afterwards that what really exasperated her was my crass stupidity. It was not my differing from her that she resented, but the fact that any human being, let alone a human being whom she looked on as moderately active-minded, should exhibit such a sub-human lack of the most ordinary pitiful glimmerings of intelligence. I do remember her saying in accents of most extreme irritation : " If I had a head like yours I should go and boil it." I was hampered by the fact that really I wasn't at all sure that I was right. That did not stop me standing up for myself with passionate self-assertion. I did, however, secretly wish that we could stop wrangling for a few seconds and give me time to work it out. My brain is never very strong on time questions, and I still never know whether the clock goes backwards or forwards when we start summer-time. Stop, of course, was the one thing we could neither of us do. Looking back on the scene it seems to me that we must have gone on arguing till exhaustion supervened had not heavenly intervention (it could have been no less, for it certainly did not come from my own brain) suddenly put into my mouth a clear, simple and lucid argument which it was impossible to withstand or contradict. That I wound up by saying, " So that's that," in a tone of most acid disagreeableness was regrettable, but almost inevitable. " Oh, I

[...] said Theodora in an immensely surprised
voice. "you're right." Then she added [...]
"Let's pretend it didn't happen." I was almost
hardly at the bottom of my heart I was quite
taken aback by being right.

In any case we had plenty of time to see the
churches at Ohrid.

Archimandrite Constantine had told us there were
three we ought to look at, Sveti Clementi, Sveti
Sofia and Sveti Jovan Kanevsky, but the first
one we found was none of these. It was a Church
of Our Lady, it was very very tiny, and it was on a
hill. There were a few not very good icons in its
small square interior, and there was a tiny garden
outside it with a border of golden wallflowers.
There was nothing whatever in it, and yet it was one
of the most moving and lovely churches I have ever
seen.

In Sveti Clementi, which is Byzantine of the ninth
century, a service was going on, so we waited a few
minutes, gazing round the warm dusky twilight
and listening to the pleasant monotonous chanting
of the Scriptures, then we went down to the hill to
Sveti Sofia. Sveti Sofia is larger than the others
and is rapidly falling into disrepair. It is unused
and shut up. There were a lot of little boys playing
in front of it, one of whom had blacked his face and
was banging a tin can. We are generally pretty
firm about small children begging ; one has to be
in the Balkans or life is not worth living, but this
was such a homelike sight, so reminiscent of London
and Guy Fawkes, that we put our hands in our
pockets. It was thus that we met the future dic-

tator of Jugo-Slavia. He had not actually got his
face blacked, but he was rather organising the
thing. I do not know his name or who he was.
He was a plain unattractive child with lumpy legs
encased in dirty white cotton socks ; he may have
been about eleven. He is, however, a born general.
He grasped the situation instantly, and sent a small
boy scuttering off for the key of the church. He
let us in and kept most of his little companions out,
which was no mean feat. He showed us over the
dim shuttered interior with bits of candle salvaged
from the iron stands. He gave us rapid and I am
sure correct explanations in Serbo-Croat, and he
did make us understand which was the refectory
and which the catacombs. When we emerged he
shooed away the yelling mob of children with which
we were at once surrounded, though after accepting
his own five dinars he looked round and indicated
the small boy who had fetched the key. His rapid
grasp of every situation, his organisation and his
peremptory way of dealing with his comrades,
several of whom were larger and older than he was,
were quite remarkable. I hope his influence in future
time will be exerted on the side of peace—I am not
in favour of a pocket Napoleon in Macedonia.

We enrolled him as a guide to Sveti Jovan
Kanevsky, and I think it was lucky that we did so,
because Sveti Jovan is not actually in the town.
It stands by itself on a small piece of rock jutting
out below the cliff. A little to the left is a tiny
fishing community, the houses half built into the
cliff, and he is, I think, a patron saint of fishing.
The church was shut, but we did not want the key.

...mountains on our left were bright in the sunshine, the green of the lower slopes was incredibly vividly bright, and the bare upper rock glows with blurred and blended colours, all of which were reflected mirror-like in the still, clear lake. On the West side, however, the lake was a pool of gold, damascened by the occasional little breezes that ruffled it, and across the fishing boats with their high prows were pulling home, leaving long furrows of brightness behind them.

The motor 'bus we were to take left Ohrid at seven the next morning. We arrived at the starting-place about ten minutes too early and the young, fair-haired porter from the hotel was plainly worried as to how to entertain us. He hit on exactly the right thing, he took us to church. It was another church that we had not seen, and I don't know if it was historically interesting or not, but it was very pleasant. Some kind of what I imagine to be a harvest service was going on. At any rate there were flowers and fruit and flat cakes lying in front of the altar screen. The cakes had votive candles stuck in them ; I don't know how the melted wax mixed with the ingredients. The service was being taken by an obvious novice. It was very interesting. Every few seconds he would forget a bit or go wrong,

117

then another bearded priest would charge out from behind the altar, whisper emphatically, and set him on the correct path again. Nobody seemed to mind, or to find themselves distracted. It was a nice service, and we were pleased to be in church ; we lighted our candles and said our short, rather vague prayer and then it was time to catch the motor 'bus.

Our first stop was Struga. All the towns we stopped at were charming, picturesque, entirely unfrequented by any kind of tourist and full of the most genuine native costumes. But though the costumes vary from town to town, it is difficult to disentangle them in one's memory. In Struga all I remember is a little girl, who may have been twelve, with a blue handkerchief over her head. Most of the peasant women, though sometimes good-looking, are rather coarse in type, and there are many traces of gipsy blood in their swarthy faces and rolling dark eyes. But this little girl and the baby brother she had in charge were flaxen fair with rosy cheeks and delicate features. She looked like the eternal heroine of all fairy tales as she stood there gazing at the motor 'bus. She might have been the third daughter, the little lost princess, the goose-girl or the shepherdess. In any case it is nice to know that she will live happily ever after.

The next stop was Debar, a wild deserted-looking village on the Albanian border. The road ran through a barren, grassy plain, on one side of which was a Mohammedan graveyard. Moslems never tend their graveyards for fear of disturbing the spirits of the dead, and this was the most desolate spot

incredibly filthy clothes.
One gipsy lady, affectionately seen off by a large family, got into the 'bus, and though she seemed to like us and kept chattering to us in Serbo-Croat or possibly Romany, we did feel that she would, in the friendliest way and with no malice whatever, have pinched any of our possessions.

The 'bus charged on and on, through lovely scenery, along the defiles of mountain passes, beside a great river. I cared less and less. We bumped about, we became rather faint and sick and exhausted. Still the 'bus charged on. We had left Ohrid at seven, breakfasting about six. At two o'clock the 'bus drew up at Mavrovo. Mavrovo is marked on few maps; travellers in Jugo-Slavia, however painstaking and indefatigable, have seldom heard of it. Only King Boris of Bulgaria, that charming and talented man, really gave it its meed of recognition. He knew all about it as soon as I mentioned it. He had found a new kind of saxifrage there in the war and Enver Pasha was born there. For us, apart from this exclusive information, it will always remain luminously memorable because there we had LUNCH. It was a good lunch too, consisting unexpectedly of roast mutton and rice pudding, and when we left the proprietor divided

an enormous bunch of cowslips, which happened to
be standing on the bar, between us.

Gostivar was one of those places which are the
essence of travel.   The day was rather grey and
cloudy, we did not get out of the 'bus.   It stood in
the middle of a very dusty irregular square, through
which ran a very muddy trickle of water.   All the
buildings in   sight   were   ramshackle   and   ugly.
Two young men in Albanian caps, rather fierce and
good-looking, their garments in a characteristically
Albanian   state   of   inconsequence   and   disrepair,
were sitting on the edge of the pavement drinking
out of a bottle.   A soldier came and had his heavy
boots, white with dust, shined up by the shoe-black,
and when the shoe-black went to get change, a
young man in a fez calmly polished up his own shoes
with the shoe-black's material.   Several little boys
hopped in and out of the filthy gutter.   One very
small person in a fez, strolled down towards us.
He had no shoes on, but he wore a very respectable
new and solid looking pair of long trousers and a
waistcoat, cut down from father's.   His hands were
in his pockets and he looked every inch a man of the
world.   He was aloof and spoke to no one ; in a
country where clothes, especially small boys' clothes,
are   just   any   old   piece   of   stuff   cobbled   up   and
incredibly patched and tattered, his magnificence
evidently weighed heavily upon him.   It was not a
picturesque scene ; it was not particularly interesting, and far from beautiful.   The 'bus stopped a
long time and we were even slightly bored.   But
fundamentally we were profoundly happy and
satisfied. There is nothing to account for it. Those

who like travel will immediately recognise the sensation, those who don't will think me mad. Perhaps we are.

I wish I could remember more about Pristina, besides I think it was the prettiest and most picturesque place at which we stopped, but it had gone from me. It had begun to rain slightly by this time, and I bought a pair of Jugo-Slav shoes for my youngest niece.

Skoplje, however, I remember well because there we had one of the largest dinners I have ever eaten. By some error we ordered both lamb cutlets and peas, and ham and eggs, and they were both so good they had to be eaten. It was swell. Also we had a bath. We hadn't had one of these since Broussa in Asia Minor some six days ago. There were other things about Skoplje ; a rather charming small monastery about five miles off ; a very superior post-office young lady who made me write out a whole telegram over again because I'd made a blot on it, to my intense anger ; an unexplained notice in our hotel saying they catered for Rotary Clubs ; some mosques and a very ramshackle, picturesque Turkish quarter ; but it was the dinner and the bath which really seemed important at the time.

And that is, as I think I said before, the pleasant thing about travelling. One's sense of proportion is so much better. One's dinner, one's bath, they block up the horizon—not an endless vista of pre-occupation with dinners and baths, but the one that happens to be with you and present. One doesn't look forward, scheming and anticipating and worrying. One goes to bed as we did that evening at Skoplje, as we did so many other evenings, well-fed, tired out and utterly contented. Sufficient unto the day has been the good or the evil thereof.

Strictly speaking I had no business to go on tour at all. I had still two more terms to run at the Academy of Dramatic Art (in those days it was not yet " Royal ") before I could consider myself a trained actress, instructed, if not proficient in elocution, miming, fencing, ballet dancing, voice-production, make-up and the actual impersonation of characters in Shakespeare and Modern Drama.

But, having heard that a certain manager was looking for a girl to play the small part of Eva in " The Private Secretary " to replace another who had fallen ill, the temptation to apply for it was too violent to resist. I do not think I ever had any illusions about the part itself. Let me state once and for all that I am a singularly poor actress, feeble of voice and constrained of gesture. I doubt very much if Bernhardt, Duse or Mrs. Siddons could have shaken the world to its foundations with Eva. But in those days I had ambitions, ambitions not to play any particular part, but simply to *be* an actress. I think what chiefly tempted me about Eva was that her lines, meagre as they were, would be spoken by me and me alone throughout all three acts.

If this does not seem to you dazzling bait, you have not been to a dramatic school. At the Academy, owing to the preponderance of male parts and the equal preponderance of female students, the heroines were always played piecemeal. A young man might strut through a whole play as Hamlet or Sidney Carton. But a young woman, fortunate enough to play Ophelia or Lucie Manette in Act 1, by the end of the play would find herself degraded to Second Clown or Assistant Executioner, a proceeding very galling to all but true-born actresses and vastly confusing to one's relatives in the audience.

So, with my knees trembling under my best frock and my head whirling under my best hat, I went to interview my first manager. As I sat in the agent's office, waiting to be summoned through the dirty, glass-topped door into the fearful presence of Mr. B., I could take no pleasure in the thought that one day my own photograph, dusty, curled at the edges and lavishly signed, might be impaled with a drawing-pin to that faded green baize board. Should I confess that I had no experience? Or should I bluff, as I had been advised to do, and refer brazenly to half a dozen imaginary engagements?

Fortunately the question never arose. Somehow, like Alice pushing through the looking-glass, I found myself on the other side of the door, and a neat, melancholy man with a large cigar, instead of asking me searching questions, was running a tape measure round my waist and hips. Still without speaking, the melancholy man removed my hat, the hat to which I had pinned so many hopes. I thought at first he was going to measure my head too, but he contented himself with pulling my body, turning my face to the light and exhibiting my teeth.

He then seated himself at a desk, wrote down some figures, compared them with other figures in a book in front of him, sighed deeply, and said, "I think you could wear Miss Davidson's clothes."

A long pause followed during which I remained standing and Mr. B. swivelling round on his chair, pulled sadly at his cigar with an air of utter abstraction. At last, turning his back on me completely, he said " I'll give you a try-out. Three pounds a week and find your own shoes and stockings."

Repressing an impulse to cry, " Oh, *thank you*, Mr. B. ! " I managed a careless, " That's settled, then ? "

I was tiptoeing towards the door when Mr. B. suddenly swivelled round again and shouted, " One minute, young lady. This is a flapper part, you know. Short skirts. Come here and let me look at your legs."

From his pocket he produced three sixpences, and pulling up my frock, inserted one between my knees, one between my calves and one between my ankles. By this time I was shaking all over, but mercifully the sixpences held firm.

" They *seem* straight," he said sceptically, lapsing once more into deep sadness. After a few more minutes of smoking meditation, it was obvious he could bear my presence no longer. Savagely pressing his bell he cried, " Rehearse King's Theatre Monday ten sharp. Send your contract on to-night."

Impelled by the sheer pressure of his hatred, I dashed for the door. It was actually swinging to behind me when I heard his voice, suave and melancholy once again, murmur, " By the way, what's your name ? "

*   *   *   *

We assembled on the night train to York where we were to open on Bank Holiday. After three weeks of rehearsal we had come to know each other's faces, but for the next six months we were to be indissolubly bound up in each other's lives. In London we had been individuals ; from the moment the train left King's Cross we became a Company—an oddly assorted company too. There was the elderly Lead, aloof yet gracious, sitting in the third-class compartment with the air of disguised royalty mingling with the common people. He was, he told us, giving Mr. B. his services for the beggarly sum of £8 a week, a mere fraction of his usual salary. But then, he confided, he was like that. If a part amused him, he did not mind roughing it. In fact, though five London managers were after him, he preferred the provinces. As for money, it was nothing to him. He was like that. The rest of us, who were not " like that " and to whom £8 a week seemed a fortune, looked impressed. All of us, that is, except the old actor with the wide hairy nostrils and the face which looked so naked without its greasepaint (there was always a rim of number nine round his collar) who played " Mr. Cattermole." " Mr. Cattermole " was fond of taking us aside and telling us how bravely the Lead clung to his vanishing middle age, how every night he anointed his scalp with bear's grease and

[illegible faded text] Mark you,
[illegible] anything [illegible] against G.," he would say
[illegible] "He's a nice old chap;
[illegible] nice old chap. But you can't fight
against poor Davina. It said to me when poor old
G. was begging with tears in his eyes for the part
[illegible] steadily worked, but he's getting a bit long
in the tooth. What about it?" And I said, 'Give
the old boy one more chance, B.' Now—if G. would
only have the guts to play character parts he might
go on for another ten years. Still it takes more than
guts to play character, it takes *talent*, my dear."
And he would inhale deeply, spreading his hairy
nostrils still wider, and throwing back his grizzled
head.

Violet Delancey always nodded vehemently when
" Mr. Cattermole " talked about the talent required
for character parts. Vi, a voluptuous frizzy blonde
of twenty-two, played the comic old housekeeper,
and had, much to her annoyance, to hide her yellow
bob under a grey wig and mar her smooth cheek
with a web of pencilled wrinkles. She had applied
for the more important of the two girl's parts and
been refused on the grounds that she was too fat to
make a convincing flapper. The very sight of
Trixie Dawson, the successful applicant with the
31-inch bust and the long slim legs, brought tears
of rage to Violet's blue eyes.

Since, for economy's sake, we were to " room "
in twos, Mr. Logan, the disillusioned manager with
the hairy tweeds and the gnarled pipe, had originally
suggested that Trixie and Violet should pair off
together. " Oh, *no*, if you *don't* mind, Mr. Logan,"

Trixie had answered sweetly, dropping her long lashes, " I'm such a little thing. I shouldn't care to be rolled on in my sleep. I'd rather room with White if you *don't* mind." Whereupon Vi, who had designs on Mr. Logan as being the most promising, as well as the most useful male in the company, whispered audibly to the A.S.M., " We all know whose room *someone* would like to share. But of course no *man* looks twice at those skinny little wurzits of women." Aloud she said, " Please yourself, I'm sure, Miss Dawson. I'm very particular too who I share with." And, arching her big bosom, she smiled at Mr. Logan, who promptly allotted her to the venerable Miss Potter.

Miss Potter, who played our chaperone on the stage and off, looked as if her only likely connection with the theatre might be selling tickets for charity performances. A seasoned, competent actress, she indulged in no stage gossip and no backbiting, and did her job as she might have done nursing, dressmaking or typewriting, simply in order to make a living. Only two things did Miss Potter really care for—gardening (though in her nomadic life she can rarely have owned so much as a window box) and the Catholic Church. She invariably wore a Liberty hat trimmed with raffia bluebells and an ebony crucifix on a black cord. On the long train journeys while the rest of us knitted jumpers or played nap, she would sit saying her rosary or marking a seedsman's catalogue.

The rest of the company consisted of two ambiguous young men in suède shoes who played the juvenile lead and the juvenile lead's best friend, an elderly young man whose face was permanently contorted in a spasm of fright (I remember neither his name, nor his part, but only a peculiar episode in which he figured in Edinburgh) and the Assistant Stage Manager, a young Jew who had an uncomfortable way of looking first at one's ankles and then running his eyes very slowly up one's body until at last they met one's own, and who wrote poetry in his spare time. I only remember one of his poems, which he thrust into my hand one wet Monday morning at Gainsborough station. It ran :

> " Dearest, you have my heart,
> Dearest, why must we part ?
> I long thee to enfold
> On a bed of gold."

Seeing my look of surprise, he hastily explained, " There's nothing personal in it. I understand you're interested in literature, Miss White. I just want your opinion—from a *purely* literary point of view."

The train journey through the stuffy August night was long and uncomfortable. I had not yet become hardened to hours of night travel, sitting, if one was lucky, in a smoke-hazed compartment ; if one was unlucky, on one's suitcase in the corridor. At six o'clock in the morning we arrived at York. My skin was taut and creeping with weariness, my powder caked with soot, my skirt rumpled and my hair like unravelled string. Moreover, it was raining. Never had the stage seemed less glamorous as I surveyed the pouched, relaxed faces ; the unshaven chins ; the filmed eyes of the actors. Violet's lipstick was smeared and her mascara streaked on her lids. Miss Potter's face showed yellow under the raffia bluebells. Only Trixie retained her porcelain neatness ; her straight flaxne hair as smooth as if it had been painted on her head and her mouth mathematically outlined with modest pink. She looked as if you had only to wipe her with a damp sponge for her to " come up " as immaculately rose and white as ever. Her travelling-costume would have been frowned on by " Vogue "—a flax-blue suit of flimsy serge, a frilly blouse, a large black lace hat and patent shoes with conspicuous paste buckles—but in my eyes at the moment she was the very nonpareil of well-dressed women.

" Come along, White," said Trixie, briskly, while I was still marvelling at her. " You and me are rooming together, so we'd better go and hunt for digs. I've got three good addresses from a boy who was with me in the ' Aunt.' "

In my ignorance I had supposed that the management would have arranged about rooms for us in each town, and that all we had to do was to inhabit them and pay for them. I rashly told her so.

" God," said Trixie, whose language sometimes fell rather oddly from her small, prim mouth, " you do have some bloody odd ideas about life on tour. Still you're only a kid beginner. Lucky I don't have to depend on you for ads. or we'd be sleeping in the police station."

Trixie was a seasoned old-timer of twenty, with two and a half years' experience " on the road " behind her. As we walked along the wet streets, tired, rain-sodden and hideously inconvenienced

By your high heels and heavy suitcases, I suggested a taxi. There was withering.

"Suppose you think you're a bloody millionaire on three quid a week? You wait till you've paid your rent and your washing and tipped the call boy and the dresser and the baggage man every Friday and you'll have a bit left over for taxis."

I fell back into silence, only muttering when I stepped in a puddle and shifted my suitcase from one aching wrist to the other.

"All the same," declared Trixie generously, two endless streets further on, "I'm glad I'm rooming with you, White. You're mad, but you *are* a lady. And that bloody fat cow Delancey definitely is *not*. And you're a Catholic, too. Funny all the women in the company are Catholics except her. Say what you like, religion *does* make a difference."

The first landlady was full up. The second had decided that never again would she take in actresses.

"I'm fed up with you professionals," she said, crossing her arms and eyeing us with great distaste, "smoking in bed and wanting hot water all hours of the night for what purpose I *don't* know."

But the third would take us in. My head was aching and I wanted sleep, nothing but sleep. Could I go to bed at once?

"You'll 'ave to wait a bit, dear," she said. "The beds isn't made yet. The two young ladies in Chu Chin Chow Number 3 only went off by the early train. Sit down and make yourselves at 'ome and Florrie'll get you a nice cup of tea."

While we gratefully drank the strong, leaf-speckled Indian tea, I took in my surroundings. They were to become very familiar, for, though we moved once and sometimes twice a week, digs varied very little. Always, except in Scotland, there were aspidistras, red serge tablecloths and photographs of seaside towns in plush frames. The great excitement was whether there would be a yellow-keyed and tinny piano for Trixie's singing exercises and whether the landlady would give us butter or margarine.

" Not used to this sort of thing, are you, White ? " said Trixie, assuming the aristocratic manner, the most genteel thing I ever hope to see. " I'm sure you come from a nice home. So do I. My mother would be *horrified* if she saw the places we have to live in. We have some really beautiful furniture. Antique. And my mother always dusts it herself. She says you can't trust the maids, though we've got three and she need never lift a finger. She's very particular, my mother. I take after her in that. D'you know I simply couldn't *dream* of sending my stockings and handkerchiefs to the laundry ? I think there's something *disgusting* in the idea of strangers handling anything so *intimate*. I *always* wash them myself. Perhaps I'm funny that way. But you're sort of sensitive. Not like that bitch Delancey. I feel you'd understand."

I did not understand then, or ever, Trixie's peculiar refinements of conduct, but I nodded sleepily. At last the landlady appeared and showed us into a dingy bedroom. As an only child who had always slept by myself I was relieved to find there were two beds. The sheets looked suspiciously grey, the mattress sagged like a hammock, but it was a bed and I was free to sleep in it.

" Give us a knock at 12.30 and a spot of lunch at one, will you ? " cried Trixie to the retreating landlady. " We've a call for rehearsal at two."

I dragged off my clothes, flung them in a heap on the floor and plunged into bed. But through my half-closed eyes I could see Trixie's pink mouth pursed in disapproval as she carefully folded each of her own garments, shook out her skirt and brushed her coat, before donning a virginal nightdress of white lawn.

" I didn't *think* you'd be so untidy, White," she said reproachfully. " Still, I'll forgive you this once. You look bloody tired, poor kid. Got that fed-up, far-from-home feeling ? "

" Mmm."

" Ah, well, it'll all come out in the wash, as the monkey said. Nighty-night." She was half in bed when she suddenly jumped out again and fell on her knees.

" Oh, damn ! " she exclaimed, " I forgot to say my night prayers. S'pose they count when you go to bed in the morning."

Exhausted as I was, I opened my eyes to watch the spectacle of Trixie at prayer. In her long white nightgown, with her fair hair in a plait and her eyes closed in an expression of unspeakable innocence, she looked exactly like Little Eva. Uncomfortably I remembered that my own prayers were unsaid. But before I could make up my mind to imitate her, I was asleep.

I woke a little later with the feeling that at least

five people were simultaneously running pins into me. As I sat up, more pins jabbed my shrinking flesh.

" Trixie," I cried.

" What the *hell's* the matter with you ? "

" Trixie, I'm being *bitten*."

Trixie was out of bed in a moment, pulling back my sheets.

" If it's bugs," she said practically, " we'll move. If it's fleas, wet soap's the thing."

We spent a quarter of an hour catching fleas with a cake of wet soap.

*　　*　　*　　*

As the weeks went by I grew accustomed to all sorts of uncomfortable things. I grew acclimatised to a diet of sausages, strong tea and grilled herrings, to living " in my suitcase," to having a perpetual smear of blue on my eyelids, to never feeling properly washed or dressed or groomed (Trixie was all these things, but I never could catch up with her), to sitting up all night in trains and playing nap at dawn in station waiting-rooms. At first I was interested in each new town we came to, would explore its streets and even the surrounding country, but soon, like Trixie and the rest, I would hardly bother to notice its name and remember only the address of that week's digs and the theatre we were playing at.

Ten people cannot be constantly in each other's society without a constant shifting of feuds and friendships. Firm alliances struck up in Macclesfield would dissolve acrimoniously in Nottingham ; people who cut each other dead in Liverpool would be found rooming together in Aberdeen.

One friendship remained constant: the partnership between the two amphibious young men, Derek and Jimmy. Occasionally Jimmy would complain that Derek had been " really rather beastly, dear," or Derek would sulk because Jimmy had snatched the corner seat twice running on night journeys, but on the whole they were a most peaceful pair. In their way, too, they were considerate. In a touring company you soon learn not to expect preferential treatment from the male members of the company. You may be the most ravishing or appealing woman in the world, but you will carry your own suitcase, fetch your own coffee from the buffet, and, if one of your fellow-actors has taken the last seat, ride from Aberdeen to Coventry in the corridor. But Derek and Jimmy, though they would not, of course, give up a corner to Trixie and myself, would hold seats for us against other claimants and, when they had quenched their own thirst, give us the dregs from their thermos flask. Sometimes the four of us would spend Sunday morning at their digs and while Jimmy played patience and Derek embroidered cushion-covers with sprays of almond blossom, Trixie (if it happened to be a piano week) would sing. She had a surprisingly good voice, high, sweet and true with a violin-like tone to it. When she was not singing indecent songs, she preferred " classical " music. Sitting very upright, like a schoolgirl practising before the headmistress and breathing very conscientiously, she would sing in her pure, sad impersonal voice :

> " One fine day you'll notice
> A ship—a ship arriving "

occasionally breaking off to snap, " For God's sake,
turn over, White," or, " Damn that bloody Wurzit of
a chord." We would all feel a little sentimental,
and tears would come into Derek's bloodshot brown
eyes. He was an odd creature, Derek, fond of
telling dirty stories in a voice as cold and greasy as
congealed bacon fat, but extremely sensitive. I
found him once sitting in the wings after the show
was over, still wearing the faded hunting pink
get-up he assumed in the last act, with the tears
running down his cheeks. He was weeping because
his landlady's little boy had caught his finger in the
mangle. Next day he spent half his salary on toys
for the child.

Once, on a Sunday journey, I found myself
marooned in a carriage with Jimmy. Jimmy was a
stocky little Jew with a straight nose and yellow
hair. Once you had heard the story of his life, how
he had been born in the East End and worked in a
hat factory, his conversation lapsed into a pale
imitation of Derek's. So, after I had giggled politely
at a few well-worn stories, I returned to my crochet
and Jimmy to his laborious spelling out of " Le
Jardin des Supplices," borrowed from and annotated
by Derek.

After about half an hour I became aware that
Jimmy had closed his book and was looking at me
wistfully.

Then, sighing and clearing his throat he said
earnestly, " Eva . . . I should like to ask you
something."

" Yes, Jimmy ? " I said, pausing in the middle of
a " treble."

Antonia White

" Well, it's something rather personal. I don't
hardly like to ask you."

My curiosity was now well aroused and I laid
down my work.

" You've always," said Jimmy, still eyeing me
with the same hungry wistfulness, " seemed to me
different from other girls, Eva. More understanding,
if you know what I mean."

Feeling just a little apprehensive, I murmured,
" What is it you want to ask me, Jimmy ? "

" I've always had an ambition, Eva. But I've
been afraid to mention it to anyone in case they'd
laugh."

Feeling on safer ground and flattered, as anyone is,
by a confidence, I said eagerly, " *Do* tell me, Jimmy."

Jimmy clenched his little ringed hands and out it
came with a rush.

" I've always been so envious of Derek. He's
such a wonderfully cultured chap. And he's so
artistic. Look at those marvellous cushion-covers
he makes. Oh, I wish I could do something like
that. Eva—I hate to bother you—but *could* you,
would you teach me to *crochet ?* "

But it was Trixie who made my first and only
tour so memorable. I have never met anyone like
Trixie, and I probably never shall again. I should
have found it difficult to live with anyone, being
bookish, moody, impractical and accustomed to
being as untidy as I liked in a bedroom of my own.
But to adjust myself to Trixie was a severe strain.
I could neither rise to her heights of old-maidish
refinement nor follow her in her moods of rollicking
relaxation. We shocked each other profoundly, we

139

quarrelled bitterly, we went for days without speaking beyond a withering, "May I trouble you for the sugar, Miss White," or "I *believe* that's my number five, Miss Dawson," yet we continued to share bed and board.

On her refined days, Trixie was a stern moralist. We would shake our heads together over the deplorable excesses of Violet Delancey who was now pursuing the stage manager so openly that, not content with tramping for miles after him in high-heeled shoes round the golf-course, she followed him home every night to his lodgings and had been found at two o'clock one morning by "Mr. Cattermole" weeping and cursing on Logan's doorstep. Yet whenever we had a free Sunday, Trixie would disappear to spend the day and a considerable part of the night with "an old friend of my mother's, dear," and arrive at the station, just in time to catch the train, in a large blue Bentley. I never saw the occupant of the Bentley, but occasionally Trixie would remark reverently, "You ought to meet my friend, White. He's really well educated," or flippantly, "Pots of money, dear, and *does* he know how to spend it? Still, all is not gold that glitters, as the monkey said." But when she returned about eleven one Sunday night and found me sitting up over the gas fire with a highly respectable cousin who had driven over from Brighton, she refused to speak to me for twenty-four hours.

Feeling unjustly treated, I taxed her as we were dressing for the show.

"Why so surly, Trixie? We were only talking and reading."

"It's the principle of the thing," she said primly, pursing up her mouth as she dipped a hairpin in a heated spoon of eyeblack and applied a blob to each long lash of her right eye. "Where's your religion, White? You know we ought to avoid the occasions of sin and to be alone with a man after dark is an occasion of sin."

"Well, there wasn't any sin," I retorted, "unless reading Herrick over a gas fire is a sin."

To my amazement, Trixie burst into tears. But practical to the last, she carefully held the lids of the made-up eye apart with her fingers so that the black should not smear.

"You and your bloody education," she sobbed furiously. "Thinking you can come it over everyone just because you went to some bloody rotten school and can read poetry."

The next day she presented me with a shilling copy of John Oxenham's " Bees in Amber."

Trixie was very devout. She went to early Mass and Communion every Sunday, even when it meant a three-mile walk before breakfast, and she wore a Miraculous Medal and three scapulars under her clothes. These last often caused her a good deal of trouble during her quick-change into evening dress in the second act. It was difficult to pin them out of sight, and she would curse them volubly, ending up with an apologetic, " Sorry, God."

One Sunday, in Edinburgh, Trixie surpassed herself in devotion. It was too far for " my mother's friend " to come, even in the Bentley, and she had the day to herself. She went, not only to early Mass, but High Mass, Benediction and Vespers as well. But, by supper time she felt ready for a little worldliness. We were in very superior digs that week, and the elderly young man with the terror-stricken face, whose part I have forgotten and whom I will call Lloyd, had a bedroom in the same house and shared our sitting-room.

On her way home from Benediction Trixie bought several bottles of Guinness. After supper she grew very merry, and dashing into our bedroom, reappeared clad only in a pair of black silk stockings and a short pink chemise.

The elderly young man looked more terrified than ever, but he was not going to be driven out of his comfortable sitting-room.

"I feel like dancing," announced Trixie gaily. "I haven't practised for months. Wonder if I can still get up on my points."

After one or two unsuccessful attempts, she balanced on the tips of her toes, a slender, charming figure. In spite of the pink chemise, her face was a study in angelic innocence.

"Wonder if I can remember a routine." She skipped a few steps, then stopped.

"Damn," she said sweetly. "I'm as stiff as a poker. Can't get my leg up. Come here, Lloyd—hold my foot."

Very gingerly, as if it had been a live shell, Lloyd took hold of the small black-stockinged foot.

"That's right. Now lift it up. No . . . higher. Hell, man, don't look so frightened. Haven't you ever seen a girl's leg before? Well, you're bloody well going to now." She whipped her foot out of

A Thoroughly Devout, Refined Girl is Sometimes
Agreeable Company.

his hand and sent it flying up in a head-high kick.
" And again—*and* again," she panted, " *now* you've
got something to write home about."

The sight of Lloyd's panic-stricken face sent her
into peals of delighted giggles. Then she relented.

" Poor lamb," she pouted. " Was he shocked
then. Did naughty Trixie commit a spot of *faux
pas?* Well, it'll all come out in the wash as the
monkey said."

Averting his eyes, the unhappy Lloyd collapsed
in a chair. Trixie sat down at the piano and,
regaining her most virginal expression, began to
sing :

> " Hark, hark, my soul,
> Angelic songs are swelling."

" You sing beautifully," said the frightened man,
" but aren't you a little cold, Miss Dawson ? "

" Trixie to you, and I'm not as cold as I look,"
cried my room-mate, taking a flying leap from the
piano stool and landing on Lloyd's knee. " I bet
you don't know the difference between a man and a
woman, Lloyd," she said, winding her slim arms
round his neck. " Sweet thirty-five and never been
kissed." And she pressed her lips to his recoiling
mouth.

After he had, with some difficulty, unwound her,
Trixie rushed once more into her bedroom and
returned with an empty Guinness bottle and a
rosary. Flinging herself on the floor and waving
the bottle in one hand and the rosary in the other,
she proceeded to pour out alternate strings of " Hail
Maries " and curses. The elderly young man, now

pale and sweating with fear, dashed out of the room and I heard the key turn in his bedroom door. After much persuasion, I induced Trixie to come to bed. Once in the bedroom, she became completely sober, did the rest of her undressing in her usual methodical way, cleaned her teeth, plaited her hair, and in her long schoolgirl nightgown, knelt down to say her prayers.

When she had finished, she opened her limpid blue eyes and looked at me reproachfully.

" You're a good sort, White," she said, " but I wish you'd take your religion more seriously. You ought to go to Communion more often."

* * * *

After six months, the tour came to an end. We had gradually declined from week-long runs in first-class towns to three nights in obscure ones. Not one of us, except the Lead, was sorry when Mr. B. wrote and said that, for the present, he had no further use for our services. We broke up one Sunday morning at Euston, with warm expressions of mutual affection and passionate promises to write. But I never set eyes on Trixie or any of them again.

The First Time I went to the North

by

EVELYN WAUGH

FIASCO IN THE ARCTIC

As soon as we crossed the Arctic circle, it grew warmer. The sun streamed through the porthole all night, making sleep difficult. At Svalbad they were selling ice-cream on the quay. At Tromso, where we disembarked, it was hotter than at any place where we had stopped since Newcastle. Most of the little towns on the way North had been dry. At Tromso there were no bars or cafés, but we were able to buy a bottle of spirits, named " 60%," which we took to our hotel. There were three of us. Hugh and I sat in our shirt-sleeves in his bedroom playing piquet and drinking " 60% " while G., who was leader of the expedition, went to see a man about a boat. That evening we took the British Consul, who was a Norwegian, to the cinema.

Next day the Government ship left for Spitz-bergen. She is a minute, very clean little steamer. She makes the journey three times in the year. The captain gave us each a glass of Benedictine on the first evening, and the mate practised his English on us. " I think your King has many children," he said. " Your Prince of Wales has no wife. The English people are greatly devoted to the Monarchy." He examined our maps and cameras and guns, our boat and our sledge which were lashed to the deck amidships. " I think you will have a very interesting expedition," he said. " You are students of science or sportsmen ? "

It was three days from Tromso to Spitzbergen, in heavy seas. There was some mail on board for the meteorological station on Bear Island, but it was too rough to put out a boat. When we reached Spitzbergen the sun was invisible behind low clouds. The cliffs were black, striped with snow like zebra-hide. We reached harbour at midnight ; sunless, grey daylight ; no one stirring ; it was as cold as an English February, no worse.

There are two coal-mines on opposite sides of the bay ; one belongs to Soviet Russia, the other to Norway. Apart from these the islands are unin-habited ; trappers have a few cabins dotted about the coast which they visit from time to time during the winter. There are no police or Government officials ; the mining company administers law and social services. There are, in the Norwegian station, four or five hundred miners and thirty or forty women. They sign on for seven years. During that time they eat and sleep in barracks, and buy what they need from the company's store. During the winter it is dark all round the clock, the harbour is sealed up and they get no mail. There is a weekly cinema and weekly steam bath ; a monthly bottle of whisky. They earn big wages and retire to Norway at the end of their seven years with sub-stantial savings unless they have lost them at poker. I met one man who had signed on three times running. He had no luck at cards. The women usually leave after three years; they make a bit too. There is an officer class of engineers who live in a comfortable mess.

But there was no one about when we landed. All we saw was an irregular street of timber buildings. It smelled a little. When we returned, after living on the ice, that was the first thing we noticed, the rank, fetid smell of human kind.

Generally speaking, there are two degrees of loneliness which affect the treatment of strangers. Communities that are fairly isolated are extravagantly pleased to see an outsider; those who are absolutely isolated find him a nuisance. We were a nuisance to the miners, but they treated us, nevertheless, with faultless courtesy.

G. had arranged for a sealer to take us up the coast to a bay on the West, where there were some huts erected by a prospecting company; they had been empty for twenty-five years, but were still in a fair state of preservation. Two previous expeditions had used them as base-store. There was still a length of rail connecting them with the beach and two or three rusty trolleys. The men from the sealer helped us land our stores and pull the boat up on to the shingle. We had provisions for about six weeks, a tent that had been used on the Everest expedition, the boat and a sledge. The plan was to work up a glacier and sledge across the inland ice to some unexplored territory on the North-East. Hugh and I were new to the North; G. had been there before.

The sealer chugged off. It was a desolate bit of shore, hung about with white fog, which sometimes

lifted to reveal three or four big glaciers flowing
down to the bay, between dark cliffs. We were on
shingle, covered in places by moss, in places by
snow. There was a small lake of fresh water behind
the huts and a stream in front. It was a nesting-
place for terns. The eggs lay all over the foreshore
in shallow little pockets of gravel ; some had already
hatched out into flappers which tumbled about at
our feet. It was difficult to avoid stepping on them ;
doubly difficult by reason of the assaults of the
mother birds which kept our attention overhead.
They hovered over us with shrill cries, lovely little
white and grey birds with long tails that shut in a
point and then flicked open in an attenuated V.
They would drop suddenly on us, pecking the crowns
of our Balaclava helmets. Sometimes three or four
would attack together, sweeping down in rapid
succession and then wheeling off, high above us.
It was not painful, but it was disconcerting. We
found the best plan, when we went to draw water,
was to carry an aluminium mess-tin on the end of a
stick. This drew their attack while we stooped
over the lake. The tins rang with the percussion
of their beaks.

It was not particularly cold. G. tried to swim,
but quickly scrambled out, blue and shuddering,
saying that it had warmed him. We spent a day
and a half repacking stores, lashing the sledge and
waxing skis. G. had said that on the coast we could
" live on the country." He and Hugh went out
with their guns but came back empty handed.
There should have been duck and ptarmigan.
" Living on the country " and telling the time by the

THE MIDNIGHT SUN.

sun are common delusions of travellers. Late the second evening we set out in the boat and rowed for two or three hours across the bay, into another smaller bay where there was another derelict hut. Seals bobbed up in the water all round us ; there were innumerable small icebergs, some white and fluffy, others deep green and blue like weathered copper, some opaque, some clear as glass, in preposterous shapes, with fragile, haphazard wings and feathers of ice, pierced by holes. The whole bay was filled with their music, sometimes a shrill cricket-cry, sometimes a sharp, almost regular metallic ticking, sometimes the low hum of a hive of bees, sometimes a sharp, splintering, sometimes a resonant boom, coming from the shore where another crag of ice broke away from the underhung glaciers. The fog cleared about midnight, the sun lay on the horizon and in the superb arctic light, that is both dawn and sunset, the ice face shone clear and blue to the white snow above it and the water was dense indigo.

The moraine of the glacier which we proposed to ascend was three miles from our landing-place ; between us lay a mosquito-infested valley of mud and sharp stones over which we had to carry the stores on our backs. We made two journeys a day, taking between thirty and forty pounds in a load. It was beastly work. On the second night we had everything we needed at the foot of the moraine. Then followed some hours scrambling up and down over the precipitous wet gravel and rocks ; at last everything was on the ice. We had been working twelve hours that day, because, in addition to the portering, we had spent most of the morning struggling to drag the boat clear of a possible high tide, with the aid of block and pulley and a series of stakes that would not hold in the loose shingle. Once on the ice, however, we felt that our worst labours were over ; we wanted to make a start and camp out of sight of the bay and the atrocious mud valley. We loaded the sledge, spread the tarpaulin covers, lashed everything firm and prepared to start. Two of us went in front harnessed to ropes ; a third stood behind holding the runners, to steer, push and see that none of the load worked loose. Tired, but light-hearted, we got into position ; G. gave the word to start. We strained forward. The sledge stood immovable as rock. The two in front had ice axes. We bent down as though starting for a sprint, drove the axes in ahead of us to pull on ; G. behind, heaved at the runners ; the sledge moved six inches and again stuck. We changed the course, striking a traverse across the slope ; we changed the traverse until it barely diverged from the horizontal. Then with the utmost labour we were able to get the thing along. We worked for two hours, tacking back and forward across the slope. At the end of that time we were spent. Our first camp lay a few hundred yards from the edge of the moraine. Next day we decided to relay the stores in two loads. In this way we travelled for a week, monotonously, working for ten hours a day and covering, on an average, about five miles.

Our difficulty, G. explained, was due to the exceptional thaw. There was never a moment when the sledge could run free. The ice was rough and hummocky, broken by rivulets, which sometimes overturned us, and sometimes necessitated unpacking, wading and repacking. The snow was soggy so that even on skis we sank in ; much of the journey was over knee-deep *levé*, a kind of fine shingle of ice pebbles. At first G. promised us better conditions when we reached the Northern slopes, but he was disappointed. It was now intensely cold ; everything got wet, tent floor, clothes, bedding, and could not be dried. Most of the time we were enveloped in white mist which rendered our direction doubtful, but whenever it cleared the prospect was magnificent. We had two Primus stoves and ate twice a day—oatmeal, oranges, chocolate, tea, biscuits and Pemican. Pemican derives its name from the dried reindeer flesh of the esquimos ; now it is factory-made specially—and, I should imagine, exclusively—for Arctic and Antarctic expeditions. It is very expensive, concentrated product of meat-fat and albumen. Its value, as revealed by chemical analysis, is stupendous. It is boiled in water, it remains suspended but undissolved, in a muddy broth ; it must be constantly stirred to prevent its settling to the bottom ; it leaves a coat of slime on spoons and dishes, which can be removed with industry. A noxious dish. Our stores also included three seven-pound tins of margarine. G. assured us that we should have a craving for fat as soon as we were on the ice. We did not find it so.

There were, however, some negative advantages of Arctic over tropical travel ; the constant light, so that one was free from the anxiety of being over-taken at nightfall with one's camp unmade ; so that instead of the twelve hours of black inactivity one could read and work without hindrance. Set against this was the fact that, however tired we were, sleep was very difficult in that bright, cold little tent. There was also the great cleanness of every-thing ; cuts healed quickly ; food remained fresh for weeks at a time ; there were no insects, no microbes and no poisons, none of that unending warfare against corruption, the sterilising and dis-infecting, the iodine and the quinine, mosquito nets and snake boots, that impede one in the tropics.

The misfortune which ended the trip came quite suddenly. We had arrived at the foot of the glacier, known as the Martin Conway, up which we hoped to penetrate into the Northern district ; it proved to be so badly crevassed that ascent was impossible. Accordingly we turned West towards the shore, where, on the banks of Wijlde Bay, G. assured us, was a trappers' cabin and a boat left by his last expedition. In dense fog we began to descend a glacier. After a time we met a barrier of rock over which it was impossible to drag the sledge. We decided to push on to the hut, carrying on our backs our beds and provisions for a couple of days. We reached the shore and slept there, the fog being too thick for us to find the way. After a few hours it lifted. We pushed on, very tired, crossed a series of shallow streams, and about three miles further of rough going on the rocky shore brought us to a wide, shallow river and beyond it the cabin. It was smaller than G. had remembered it, the size of a *wagon lit* and extremely dirty. A single bunk gave accommodation for two lying feet to head ; the third slept on the floor. In six or seven hours we awoke. A brief survey convinced us that G.'s boat was not there. We decided, however, to make the cabin our headquarters for the time and explore the surrounding hills, none of which had been mapped. Hugh and G. set off for the sledge to bring back further supplies, while I was left to get the cabin into order. I swept it clean of refuse, chopped up some driftwood that lay on the beach, cleaned the little stove, lay down on the furs that covered the bunk and fell asleep again. I was wakened by G., who was in a state of some agitation. Gradually, as we waded the river and tramped back up the bay, I gathered what had occurred. He and Hugh had got to the head of the bay, where they discovered that the series of little streams which we had crossed a few hours before had suddenly changed to a tearing flood. Hugh was a heavyweight boxer, of greatly superior physique to either G. or myself. He had managed to cross, but G. had been driven back. He had gone on to the sledge. It was certain he would not be able to get back to us, loaded, without assistance.

For half an hour before we reached it, we could hear the roar of the flood. When finally we stood on the bank the sound was so great that we could barely make ourselves heard, shouting in each other's ears. The flow was terrific, of no great depth as yet, and still divided by shingle banks into four or five streams, but running at a dizzy speed, full of boulders and blocks of ice, whirling down in it.

G. and I tied ourselves together round the waist. The climbing ropes were on the sledge, but we had found some tarred twine in the cabin which provided us with a treble length of about a dozen paces. First one of us waded in, the other paying him out from the shallow water. Half way across the stream came to our middles and it was impossible to stand without the support of the cord ; when the first was in shallow water, he pulled the other across ; the cold was so intense that we did not feel the ice-blocks that pounded against us. In this way we reached the final channel. Hugh was already in sight with a laden pack. We threw him the string on a ski-stick and managed to drag him across. Then we began the return journey. At the last channel, after G. had got across, the twine broke in several places. Hugh and I were swept down, tumbled over and over. I had time to form the clear impression that we were both done for, when I found myself rolling in shallow water and was able to crawl ashore. Hugh was stuck on a small iceberg in midstream. There did not seem to be any way of helping him. We shouted to him to throw away his pack. But he got to his feet and came across, fully loaded. Uncertain memories of how we got back to the hut. At one time we seem to have rubbed one another with sand to get back our circulations. Our jaws were out of control, set tight with cold or chattering, so that we could not speak. Eventually we got into our sleeping-bags and slept. Our watches had been broken in the flood so that from now onwards we had no means of telling the time. We do not know how long we slept. When we awoke we found we could scarcely move from stiffness and bruises. Hugh had come off the worst with a badly swollen knee. For about twenty-four hours we lay in the cabin, two on the bunk, one on the floor, alternately dozing and investigating our injuries. Then we began to review our situation. G. said that the flood was temporary, due to the bursting of some ice-dam in the hills. When we felt better he and I hobbled up and found it deeper and stronger than before. It seemed clear that it would only cease with the thaw. Hugh could not possibly move for some days. We had pemican and paraffin for three days' normal rations, enough to support life on for a fortnight or more. The trapper was not due at his hut for about a month, when he would probably arrive to revictual for the winter. There were three plans open to us; to attempt another crossing of the river to the sledge, to wait in semi-starvation for the return of the trapper, to abandon the sledge and tent and attempt a journey over the ice, behind the river to our original base, where we had left stores and the boat. All had abundant disadvantages. The decision depended largely upon Hugh's knee. We cut down rations to a subsistence basis and waited four days. Then he proclaimed himself able to walk. We took our beds and the remains of the provisions and tramped slowly to the river. It was worse than ever. We were still suffering from the effects of our previous crossing and weak from four days' under-feeding; with packs and without a line we should clearly never get across. G. maintained a pathetic belief in the abatement of the flood, but Hugh and I knew that this was its normal condition and that we had found it passable on the first morning only by reason of some ice block higher up, forming a momentary dam. G. wished to build a turf cabin and wait for another occurrence of the same kind. Hugh and I voted for the mountain journey. I did not think it would be successful, but it seemed preferable to waiting. This essay might be called " the first time I despaired of my life." In fact, we did the journey in three days, without an adequate map, without tent, climbing rope, ice axes, crampons, with half a bowl of pemican once a day as our only ration. I might also have called this article " the first time that I felt really tired."

The First Time I Discovered that the Past was Real

by

ARTHUR BRYANT

I HAD never travelled before in the realms of gold. At school I had loved history in a desultory sort of way, but never seriously enough to impress either myself or, with one exception, my school-masters. My chief acquaintance with the past had been a meticulous knowledge of the details of Napoleon's campaigns, learnt with the aid of a set of Halma men and the diagrams of battlefields in Alison's "History of Europe," that stupendous work in ten volumes which proves, as Disraeli put it, that Providence was on the side of the Tories. Then came the war with its ceaseless transfers and comings and goings, little conducive to the study of history—and thereafter the post-war Modern History School at Oxford, which a cynic might claim was even less so. After that, being at that stage of my life a theoretical "Socialist" with an unorthodox itch to practise what I preached, I taught such text-book history as I had to bright-eyed little boys in an L.C.C. school, till the authorities with delicious illogicality brought these labours to an end by making me the Principal of a Technical College.

But after two years of supervising classes in draw-ing from the life, art metal-work, motor engineering, book-keeping, plumbing, mothercraft and home-dressmaking, the generosity of an ancient Cheshire house to whom I had become akin put into my hands the stuff of which history is made. Put into my hands is a misnomer, for it would have required a giant's hands to have clasped at once all the Shakerley papers. One grey December day in 1923, a concealed door in the wall of the Somerford library, decorously camouflaged by an eighteenth-century hand with the names of books that were never written—Bishop Allworthy's *Sermons*, Lear's *View of the Stage*, Dr. Maggott on *The Hereafter*—was opened for me and I found myself standing in a vast stone cell, with shelves all round me loaded with almost all that remained of the life record of countless Cheshire men and women. I did not, of course, know this at the time ; all I saw were bundles and bundles of documents, tied in dirty grey parcels, and on tables round the walls an indescribable litter of parchments and papers. There were also some great seals of England lying about on chairs as though they were waiting to be thrown away as too old to keep. And the whole floor was powdered fine with the dust of broken seals.

Such was my first introduction to the Shakerley MSS. As casually I began to turn a few of the papers over, something of their meaning came dimly to me : here was the actual past, of which I had read unimaginatively in books. I could touch it and peer into it and savour its musty, faint but vivid perfume. Curiosity gripped me.

After my first discovery, I asked to be made free of the muniment room. Every day during that Christmas holiday, I turned the great silver key, pushed back the heavy door and then closed it after me and there sat down in that cold storage chamber of the past. The living life of the house without, the misty trees in the park and the sodden landscape of wintry Cheshire beyond receded : I could only hear the whispering voices of men and women who after the silence of centuries had found a listener and were trying to speak. And gradually I learnt to attune my unaccustomed ears.

At first I did little more than follow an idle curiosity, picking up such letters as lay on the surface and tasting rapidly wherever the unfamiliar handwriting admitted of such easy reading. For the most part the papers had been untouched ; successive generations of family solicitors had occasionally entered to search for some ponderous conveyance or will, but had never attempted to penetrate further. Once an eighteenth-century antiquarian had busied himself for a short while among the papers, and some traces of his intrusion—a letter or two to the Shakerley who then owned Somerford and an occasional scrawl of indication on the back of some document or parcel—betokened his limited interest. Since that time a herald or a local antiquarian had on rare occasion made his entry to pursue momentarily some particular search, heraldic or genealogical, leaving behind him an untidy trail of rummaged papers. And the last of Somerford's chatelaines, a woman of character and intelligence, had spent some curious hours, as many as ill-health and a crowded life of many activities admitted, pursuing some long-forgotten theme of family history. But systematic search

there had never been ; the early Historical Manuscript Commissioners had not set foot in Somerford—
probably they had been roughly repelled by the
spoilt, ill-tempered aristocrat who, surviving from
the heyday of the Regency into the decorous order
of Victorian England, had closed the doors of Somerford to all but dancing girls and his own protégés.
The great bulk of the Shakerley papers lay as
they had lain for centuries.

What began as a relaxation from the monotony
of a winter holiday in a lonely country house soon
became a regular hobby, and when I returned to
my professional labours in southern England I
took a few of the bundles with me and fell into the
pleasant habit of occupying my evenings by copying
the more interesting parts of the letters they contained into a large exercise book which I bought
for the purpose. When Easter again released me, I
hurried North to renew my acquaintance with the
muniment room, silent and unvisited during my
three months' absence—that tiny pin-point of time
in its long generations of oblivion. The letters I
had copied during my absence had aroused my
curiosity to pursue a dozen different trails, and my
blood was whetted for the chase. I began to undo
bundle after bundle to discover what each contained, and whether they could assist my searches.

Many of the bundles, I soon found, revealed only
legal documents, long disused, the titles to land in
Cheshire and Lancashire villages of homely names,
some of which, however, during the nineteenth
century had grown into household words of semi-
humorous, wholly industrial connotation, but which

at the time referred to in these documents had been merely rustic and local. Many of these deeds were of almost terrifying antiquity—tiny slips of parchment, beautifully written in Latin in hands reminiscent of the more individual examples of modern script and in far finer preservation than their eighteenth and nineteenth-century successors. There seemed at first something uncanny in turning over and fingering conveyances of land in places like Stockport, Wigan and Macclesfield, made in days when King Henry II. sat on the throne of England and whose minute pendant seals bore the devices of long-vanished monasteries and of semi-fabulous beings like the seven palatine Earls of Chester. Others, taking up as much cubic space as a hundred of their forerunners, when unfolded presented thick sheet after sheet of closely writ parchment of apparently prodigious importance, but examined proved to be only some cumbersome eighteenth-century will or marriage settlement. For the lawyers, who in days of universal illiteracy had secured their craft monopoly by the simple device of being able to read and write, had learnt to preserve it, as the nation became literate, by ingeniously constructing a wordy jargon, which no man but themselves could understand and which they ever expanded as the march of human reason toiled vainly after them. All this, which others learn from books or teachers, I came to discover for myself.

But what I sought and learnt to treasure were not the deeds. The jewels that lay thick to my delving hands were the letters still folded as their long dead recipients had left them, the very sand from the sand-dishes of their first writers glittering in their folds, so that often my fingers and wrists were stained with a minute dust. Sometimes I found them in hundreds, tied into parcels by some impatient solicitor or agent and marked omnisciently "Of no importance." I learnt to value these indexes of the barren precision of the legal mind, for they pointed me to my richest veins of gold. At other times I would come unexpectedly on letters buried deep in bundles of conveyances, whose context seemed to have no connection with theirs. I learnt to seek for them in all places ; pressed between the pages of account or housekeeping books, trodden underfoot beneath the dust of the broken seals on the stone floor, thrust into corners of cupboards or patching the mouldered lids of deed-boxes. Then I would unfold them and with excitement peruse their contents.

Those were the days of the first chase ; I pursued wildly and scarcely knew what I pursued. My quarry, I came to learn, needed staider hunting. A casually opened letter would give a glimpse of some—to me—thrilling intimacy, a Jacobean elopement, the scapes of an Elizabethan undergraduate, a harassed Governor of Chester receiving royal orders from James II. to admit a priest to say mass in defiance of law in Chester Castle. One jumped wildly to conclusions, but soon found oneself checked and the scent lost. For a time I was content to follow some other trail, where so many presented themselves, but the check was always repeated. Curiosity, and something quietly insistent inside me, in time prompted to a more laborious pursuit. Patience, method, above all industry, these plainly were the *desiderata* for the discovery of what I was seeking.

They came to my aid. The work was so absorbing that they grew on me imperceptibly. It was not till the last hour struck in the history of Somerford and the great house, dismantled, opened its doors to a barbaric invasion of antique dealers and auctioneers before its final agony at the hands of the estate breaker—product characteristic of our petulant, uncreating age—that I was able to survey the full scope of the work before me. Then the papers, in vast wooden boxes and trunks, were moved to their new home in Buckinghamshire, where humbler but even older doors opened to receive them. And here, in a room whose walls had shadowed Elizabethans, the vast array of the Shakerley MSS. was spread day after day on the unswept floor, despite the protests and entreaties of womankind—" worse enemies to papers " as one of Pepys' correspondents described them, " than rats and mice." Yet, now that I recall it, it was one of that destructive sex who knelt beside me on the floor night after night as together we turned over countless papers, ever sorting and arranging till all lay in the neat folders prepared for them.

Each year from 1560 to 1850 had its own folder (the deeds which strayed back into the misty antiquity of the twelfth century were arranged separately according to their nature or topographical context) ; each letter spread out took its exact chronological place in the year file to which it belonged. Nearly all the letters were folded as they had first been sent, the old practice till the coming of envelopes in the early nineteenth century being elaborately to fold the single or double sheet on which the letter had been written, seal it across the open fold and address it on the back : many of the missives so made were no bigger than a book of stamps. Only the extreme quality of the old hand-made paper on which they were written had preserved them against cracking along the folds and so falling to pieces. It was noticeable that the nineteenth-century letters were mostly in far inferior condition to those of the seventeenth—an alarming thought for the would-be Horace Walpoles of this age, especially when it is remembered that the paper on which an English gentleman of 1850 corresponded with his friends was of infinitely superior quality to that used to-day. Yet in many cases it had become of vital importance to unfold the manuscripts and lay them flat if their continued preservation was to be assured.

Dating was not always an easy matter. Many of the letters were undated, and had to be fitted into their proper place by their context, which was rather like doing a jigsaw puzzle with half the pieces missing, for of course much material that might have guided one had long ago perished, while the correspondence as a whole tended like that of nearly all country house collections, to be rather one-sided, the outgoing letters reposing, if at all, in the muniment rooms of their recipients' descendants. Here the calendars of the Historical Manuscript Commissioners and of the various learned societies who have published works on family papers proved helpful ; the indexes perused would often reveal a Shakerley, a Buckworth or a Vernon, whose letter fitted neatly into some vacant niche in the Shakerley collection. More often there was nothing to guide us and we had to keep a number of spare folders roughly dated into which we cast doubtful letters according to such broad characteristics as style and handwriting, there to wait until I became sufficiently familiar with the tiny intimate allusions they contained to date them with greater certainty.

Yet, though there was much delving in the dark and at first a good deal of the usual misdating consequent upon the confusing habit of our forbears of dating their Lenten letters sometimes according to the old style and sometimes the new— it is striking how often even the learned editors of the Historical Manuscript Commission Reports have fallen into this easy fault through not paying sufficient attention to the *minutiæ* of the context— there were other factors, familiar to all who work on records, which lightened one's labours. The old practice of addressing letters on the back of the paper on which they were written almost invariably enabled one to identify the recipient as well as the sender, a thing that would have been almost impossible under the modern usage of separate envelopes, which are usually consigned after opening to the waste-paper basket. Another great boon was the pre-nineteenth century custom of attaching surnames to uncles, aunts and cousins : Uncle Shakerley of Gwersylt is a far more recognisable character to the historian than Uncle George. Against this must be set off the minor inconvenience of finding a man's " in-laws " described by the same style impartially as the closer kinship of father, mother and brother. And, until one became used to it, it was often confusing to find intimate friends and lovers concluding their letters : " Your humble and obedient servant," while tax-gatherers and other officials almost invariably ended their unpalatable communications with " Your loving friend."

After about 1670 elementary postmarks, at first of date alone (though of the day and month only and not, unfortunately, the year) and later sometimes of place of posting, often proved useful. Nor was the occasional help to be obtained from the armorial devices on the beautiful red seals to be despised.

When at last the letters were all sorted and the year files placed in a vast oak spice-chest with innumerable drawers (made by a Welsh carpenter for the writer of many hundreds of them in the early eighteenth century), the education of an historian had begun. A chance curiosity had grown into a holiday task, and a holiday task now became the regular routine of every evening and leisure day. Each night, when I came home and the lamps were lit, I unlocked the spice chest, pulled out the particular folder on which I was working and transcribed or calendared, as the interest or reverse of the particular document dictated, letter and bill. Sometimes months would elapse before some particularly bulky folder, containing many hundreds of letters, could be disposed of. At first I transcribed by hand with a tall feather pen which seemed appropriate to my subject, but as I became wiser I learnt to prefer a typewriter, which by enabling me to take carbons saved me much wearisome cross referencing and gave me files of transcripts arranged under subject as well as date. The sweet and regular labour of it taught me what school or university—though they laid the foundations of it—had never taught, a craft ; to do one thing thoroughly without evasion or omission. It is a lesson learnt by most men who practise a handicraft in their own way, but seldom provided by the rather " slap-dash " and desultory general reading of modern literary education. Yet it is well worth attaining, for though it may not increase a man's moral stature, it tends to give him a sense of balance and of values, makes him love quality and shun shoddy, and teaches him to judge men and things by a proper valuation.

This is a digression, but I feel that I owe too much to the Shakerley MSS. not to record that debt. The play's the thing. And the play, if there was much labour in it, was none the less all delight. The interest of slowly unfolding the course of one human life after another, with all its desires and aspirations, its joys and pathetic failures, was such that only a very dull man could have failed to be absorbed. And here were real lives that had once meant as much to their possessors as mine to me. One got a queer almost godlike sense of being able to see the future of these long dead beings as well as the past, of being able to feel and yet to be unswayed by feeling, and with it a sense too of great humility, for even as one now beheld these, so might one also be seen and judged hereafter. Something of the quality—emotion recollected in tranquillity—which Wordsworth held to be the essential of poetry was present in those silent hours of the night, looking over the shoulders of those far writers and tracing in equally transient shadow on the wall of one's own age the words they wrote.

The variety in the human interests revealed by the papers was almost endless. In various queer ways, at least a dozen correspondences of different Cheshire, Lancashire and North Welsh families had found their way into the general body of the Shakerley MSS., and each started some new pursuit. One, which gave me intense excitement at the time but led to no capture, was a collection of letters and documents belonging to that Fitton of Gawsworth who was the father of Mary Fitton, the elusive being whom some have claimed as the Dark Lady of the Sonnets. Suppose, I hazarded, I should come across some allusion to this suspected, lost relationship ; suppose even—but that was hoping too much ! Yet sometimes I wonder whether in some unexamined collection of papers somewhere in the Midlands, a bundle of letters may not one day be unearthed bearing Shakespeare's signature. There were so many unsuspected things lying among these Shakerley papers, of whose existence till a few years ago no one in the world was aware, that nothing of that kind would ever surprise me.

Many were the delightful vistas down which one gazed as one pursued one's task. I recall one such, glimpsed at the moment when I had just moved the MSS. to their new home. My neighbour and land-lord, Sir Harry Verney, sent me as a welcoming gift a copy of the first and best of all printed country house collections, the "Verney Memoirs," whose originals were, and still are, housed in Claydon House a mile or two away. I read them with delight and was particularly enchanted with the character of that prince of seventeenth-century letter-writers, Tom Verney, the "importunate beggar," for whom, as an American wrote with truth "nature had not broken the mould in which Falstaff was run." Stimulated and enthused, I opened one of the boxes of Shakerley MSS. that had just arrived from Cheshire and took a handful of letters out at random. To my amazement almost the first I opened was a neat missive signed Tom Verney and addressed to that warm-hearted, irascible cavalier, old Sir Geoffrey Shakerley, the Governor of Chester Castle. It proved to be just such a letter as I had learnt to expect from honest Tom, urging in super-lative and almost undeniable eloquence the pros-pects of some primitive mining venture on which he was engaged on Sir Geoffrey's Welsh lands ; nor did it fail to conclude with a tear-raising request for a loan of £3. Thirty years had elapsed since Tom Verney had written the last of the begging letters quoted in the "Verney Memoirs," but here he was still at his old game and with gusto undiminished for all his three score years and ten. I hurried down to Claydon House to verify the handwriting by Tom's letters there : the identity was unmistakable. And as the £3 had been duly loaned by Sir Geoffrey and almost certainly never repaid, I amused myself by calculating how much the present head of the house of Verney owed the present head of the house of Shakerley. At compound interest I think it worked out at about half a million.

The personalities whom I learnt to know and grew to love, as I copied their letters by my own fireside, gradually became more real to me than any of my own contemporaries. They lived for me, and still live, just as Elizabeth Bennet and Mr. Micawber and Colonel Newcome and all that glorious company live for lovers of books, only with the enhanced vitality of having once been actually alive. The two Yorkshire sisters, for instance, one of whom, in 1628, married a Cheshire squire and the other a Lothbury merchant of the house of Lowther—" I hop to God I have got an onast religas man," wrote the latter on her wedding day—who used to end their letters to each other with touching formality :

> " I leave you to God and rest
>   Your true loveing sister till deth."

Yes ; and after death ; the sweet piety of the home on the Yorkshire moors that bore that love still shines through the faded ink and has power to touch the reader after more than 300 years. " Sweet sister, I have sent you a little suegar lofe : I pray you accept of it, tho' it be but small. I left behind my lute," she adds, " it is in a canvis bag upon the bed in the best chamber."

I remember one letter that gave me particular pleasure. It was from a small boy at school to his guardian, and written in the year 1700 :

"Honored Sir,—

"I received your cloaths you sent me : they are a little to long but that is no fault and a little thing makes the goold buttons being worne before to unravel and Maddam Thellwall thinks they are too good to spoil and advises me to keepe them till Christmas againe, and to wear the cloaths with silver olive buttons, and sais a frise would have been much better for every day, for all the boys that are Gentlemens sons wear them, for it is so cold, and are very cheaper.

"I was not well but have taken fisik. One day I was taken in the Scoole with the griping of the guts, which Mr. Prise thinks to be the wormes. No more at present but my seruis to your Lady from him who is

"Your humble servant
ROGER BRADSHAIGH."

Dearest, I think, of all the dead men and women I grew to care for was Peter Shakerley. The old man still beetles at me from under his great Hanoverian wig in the gold frame above the table where I write ; the house he built in his old age was where I found the Shakerley papers, and, though it is now perished and the tall trees he planted all felled, his careful, farseeing spirit still broods over the wasted parklands of Somerford and in the little panelled chapel which alone survives of the ordered paradise he created in what was formerly a wilderness and has now by man's greed and folly been made a wilderness again. Yet Peter was not always old. Once in his youth he stampeded, to his father's fury, through the slow formalities of a marriage settlement ; "we had much ado," wrote his

179   M 2

delighted father-in-law (who had gained greatly by his impetuosity) " to keep him from kissing his bride before matrimony was all read." The tender and beautiful woman he took to himself so gallantly that day gave him sixteen years of happiness, but no children, and more than twice that time of loneliness after her early death.

Yes ; it is easy to love Peter Shakerley—the bold sloping writing so full of strength and character, the terse, manly style—" so," he wrote to his erring undergraduate ward, " I shall judge of your devotions in the future by the balance remaining in your hands at the end of each quarter "—the splendid virility that could cause him at the age of seventy to issue a challenge to two relations, thirty years younger than himself, " to undertake me either at shooting, angling or walking " during a stormy March holiday upon the Derbyshire moors. And most of all, one loves him for his work, treasured up in that great legacy of papers he collected and left behind— the record of a life spent in the service of his country and his neighbours, ten years a soldier and Governor of Chester, twenty-five years a member of Parliament, corresponding voluminously with his constituents on every aspect of the trade and rising industry of the third commercial city of England, faithful executor and trustee of half a dozen of the great estates of Cheshire and Lancashire, two at least of which he saved from destruction and ruin.

No man can live for ever ; neither can his work. To read the lives of the ancient dead over their own shoulders is to con that mournful lesson ; they lived, desired, and strove,

" And all their hopes and all their fears
  Are bygone things of other years."

Yet, as I read, I found that even that had in it
some sense of quiet satisfaction and companion-
ship ; the gulf of loneliness that divides man from
man is bridged in that enchanted moment ; one
knows the nature of one's lot on this dream-visited
planet, and accepts it with all its implications :

" I know my life's a pain and but a span.
  I know my sense it mock'd in everything ;
  And to conclude, I know myself a Man—
  Which is a proud and yet a wretched thing."

The First Time I Turned Professional

by

DOREA STANHOPE

"THE child is musical," said the family. " She shall have piano lessons." Dimly I can remember a sad house in St. John's Wood where a man with a drooping moustache listened every Friday afternoon to a penance of inaccurate scales and mishandled exercises which I had made no attempt whatever to practise during the previous week. Eventually he retired—or died—and my musical training was continued by a ferocious woman who, remarking that I was web-fingered, presented me with an appalling little contraption made of corks and wire ; a cork was placed in between each of my fingers and, encouraged by the statement, " Beethoven permanently injured his left hand by doing this," I was made to clench both fists—with extreme pain and little result. Finally, absolved from struggling with the gigantic chords by which sonatas, symphonies and scherzos are created, I was left to tamper with the lesser works of obscure, modern composers from Central Europe who had written so many discords into their " fantasies " that the numerous errors in execution on my part made little difference to the general musical effect. All the same it was an unsatisfactory state of affairs. There was a piano, and I wanted to play on it ;

but the endless practising and building up of technique before any sort of fluency could be obtained was altogether too much trouble for my lazy soul.

One happy day I came home with a new piece of music. The front page was decorated with a highly coloured picture of an Arab on horseback, a yellow-ochre desert and a preposterous mauve sunset. Written in blood-red letters across this masterpiece were the words " Sand-Dunes. Fox-trot." It was a melancholy tune in C minor— I can remember it to this day—but it served its purpose. From that moment all ideas of serious piano playing flew to the winds and jazz rhythm became imbedded into my whole system. It was not altogether popular so far as my more aged relatives and friends were concerned. The sound of dance music, whether played solo or by a full band, is astonishingly disagreeable to the majority of elderly ears. One can understand the intense dislike of " hot " music—especially when the trumpets and saxophones leap into some devilish improvisations on an already unlovely theme— but why be so vindictive about it all ? " Those awful crooners. . . ." " That dreadful jazz. . . ." " It ought to be stopped. . . ." I may be pre-judiced, but I find a saxophone solo infinitely preferable to the Albert Hall Sunday afternoon altitude competitions between coloratura and flute.

Badly bitten myself by the jazz bug, I promptly infected three of my friends with the same disease. A saxophone, banjo and set of drums were bought and we amused ourselves for hours regardless of the complaints which were hurled through telephone and letter-box by exasperated neighbours. Eventually the " good workers " of charity organisations and welfare committees got to know about us, and requests began to arrive for our services for every conceivable kind of entertainment and function. I will not bore the reader with a long description of our apprenticeship in syncopation. It is sufficient that we jazzed our way through variety shows, flower shows, baby shows, mothers' meetings, Conservative, Socialist and Liberal tea-parties, jumble sales, concerts, bazaars and dances in every town hall and church room in Outer London. And the pianos ! Some were untuneable ; others inaudible. Sometimes a few notes would stick down ; occasionally a loud pedal jammed ; once a whole keyboard split. How I used to long for a multi-millionaire crazy enough to buy up all the dilapidated pianos in town halls and church rooms and replace them with new Steinways. . . .

At the end of two years we paused for reflection. It wasn't such a bad little band and we had learnt quite a lot. When required the banjoist could switch over to the Hawaiian guitar, and the saxophonist managed a solo or two on the clarinet. We had picked up a second pianist. In an Edinburgh back kitchen I had received some sound instruction on the drums, and at Cannes had been shown how to make music by drawing a violin bow across the flat edge of an ordinary saw. (Incidentally this created something of a sensation and was responsible for a request audition at the B.B.C. Rather over-elated with myself, I sat in a richly

draped studio at the old Broadcasting House at
Savoy Hill and gave what seemed—to me—to be
a most moving interpretation of " The Londonderry
Air." With one accord headphones were flung
down, lights flashed on and off, doors were opened
and pale young men turned even paler. " *Thank*
you," they said. " That is *quite* sufficient. You
will hear from us." But I never did. . . .)

By this time, the North, South and East Ends of
London seemed fairly satisfied with us as an amateur
band. Why not have a shot at playing profes-
sionally in the West End ? Instead of being invited
as guests to private dances, why shouldn't we be
engaged as professionals to provide the music ?
We were up against several difficulties—the fact
that we were women being the biggest of all. It
was understandable, I suppose. In cafés and
cinemas, on piers and music-hall stages, women's
bands are gloomily accepted, in spite of their
unsmartness and a dogged determination sooner or
later during every performance to play the " 1812 "
symphony—with coloured lighting effects. But
four young women playing at London dances
during the season was a very different state of
affairs. " Oh, my God, a female band. Let's
go to the Berkeley." That was the attitude to be
fought against. Besides, it wasn't " done " for the
" daughters of Society "—as the *Gloucester Echo*
once so kindly christened us—to enter the dance-
band profession. Incidentally, some of the Press
notices took a great deal of living down. " Society
saxophonists. . . ." " Four Society girls have
discovered a novel way of earning their own living

and . . . have turned themselves into the Bandits
Jazz Band." Cruellest of all was an extract from
Truth. " A great economy is to be made in the
matter of the band. Instead of the usual kind, which
rarely costs less than thirty guineas and makes a
great deal of fuss about that—the Bandits Dance
Orchestra is to perform. The Bandits consist very
largely of the nieces of well-known people."

Our first engagement was to play for the staff
dance of Fortnum and Mason. It was not a successful début. We arrived to find the whole of the
first floor cleared for dancing and, accurately
placed in the very centre of this huge space, some
forlorn chairs and a lonely upright piano. Very
upright that piano looked and very disagreeable,
as much as to say, " Why have I been left in the
middle of the room like this ? I'm one of the Broad-
woods, you know." (Which reminds me, quite
inconsequently, of the disastrous end to a certain
dinner party given many years ago by my grand-
parents. The guests included a director of one of
the largest piano manufacturing companies and his
wife. She was a very smart and charming woman,
but she could not bear to be connected in any way
with the—to her—derogatory trade of piano-
making. To ensure a successful party the other
guests had been warned of this complex and implored
on no account to bring the word " piano " into
the conversation. All went well ; the dinner was
consumed without any unfortunate reference to the
forbidden subject ; bridge had silenced any further
small-talk. At last the guests prepared to leave
and their cars were ordered. My grandmother,

triumphant that the evening had passed off successfully and elated that the nervous strain was over at last, was heard to say in clear and bell-like tones, " Oh, Mrs. So-and-So, your *piano* is at the door . . .") But to return to the scene of our début as a professional dance band. We started to tune. Quavering sounds that resembled no recognised note on any musical scale emerged from the saxophone ; the " A " string of the banjo suddenly took fright and snapped with the squawk of a scared hen ; a cymbal slipped out of a shaky hand and crashed to the ground. Things looked—and sounded— bad, but far worse was to follow. To compete with the size of the room and the number of dancers we had engaged an extra saxophonist for the evening. (In the happy-go-lucky fashion of amateurs it had not occurred to us that there are good, bad and execrable dance musicians. To our inexperienced minds it was only sufficient to go to a dance band agency and demand a saxophonist much in the same way as one would order a car from the Daimler Hire Company.) From the very start there was something wrong with that man's appearance. As soon as he arrived our comforting vision of an impeccably dressed, shiny haired, top-of-the-tree professional vanished. He was old and very bald, and his dinner-jacket would have shamed the most disreputable scarecrow. " Never mind," we murmured to each other. " He looks so funny that he's probably a genius," and full of hope and trust we took him round the corner to Sovranis for a drink before the party started. That drink settled matters once and for all. He patted each of us on the back

in turn and wheezed fatherly advice into our ears.
" Don't you ladies worry about to-night. You leave
it all to me. Whatever happens remember that I'm
the melody. I play the tune and all you have to
do is to follow me." Before the second dance had
finished it was obvious that what little ability our
friend possessed on the saxophone had been drowned
in whisky. There was only one thing to be done.
Before his condition became too noticeable he had
to be removed from the building. The difficulty
was to get him away quietly and without a scene.
We tried persuasion. (" I can't leave you ladies.
I'm the melody.") We tried threats and abuse.
(" Yes, I'm rotten at fox-trots, aren't I ? Let's
play a waltz. Let's play ' Millions of 'arlequins.' ")
In despair we explained matters to the heads of the
firm and a few minutes later the staff of that Pic-
cadilly store was vastly amused to see two of their
largest and strongest directors acting as " chuckers-
out " to one of the band. Hours later, when the
party had finished and we were starting for home, a
lonely figure was found outside the main entrance
of the shop. He was leaning heavily against several
hundred pounds worth of plate-glass window and
murmuring sadly to himself, " I can't leave . . .
I'm the melody. . . ."

   In spite of that lamentable first effort we started
to book up engagements and were soon playing
three or four times a week. Taking it all round, it
was extraordinarily hard work. People have the
idea that a dance musician doesn't get up till
lunch-time and even then has nothing to do till
after dinner. Believe me, that is a pure hallucina-

tion. Every other morning we rehearsed from 10.30
till one o'clock. (We had to keep our programme
up to date, and the average life of a dance tune is
about a month.) More often than not it was a
bleary-eyed, angry quartet that turned up, having
played practically non-stop for five or six hours
through the previous night, but whatever state of
exhaustion and bad temper we arrived in, it was
impossible not to laugh most of the way through
those rehearsals. The sitting-room of my flat
measures exactly 13 feet by 10 feet, and most of the
floor-space is already covered by a grand piano, two
large arm-chairs and a sofa. A big drum, two music
stands, three dining-room chairs, a saxophone,
piano, accordion and banjo, and seven or eight
human beings were also fitted into that room on
rehearsal mornings. Don't ask me how it was done.
I can only imagine that, looking up from the street,
passers-by could see the outer walls of that poor
little sitting-room bulge and contract to music in
the same way as one watches whole houses behave
in a Walt Disney film.

Certainly there is no monotony in the dance-band
profession. We seemed to be perpetually piling
ourselves and our instruments into cars and moving
around from place to place. I can remember one
week which was particularly varied in engagements.
First, a big charity ball at the Hyde Park Hotel.
Then two afternoons at a spring fashion show at
Harvey Nichols. They weren't easy afternoons
either. Not only had we to play for an hour and
a half without pause, but also without comment
owing to loud speakers being installed throughout

. . . Some Deplorable Country Dances.

the shop. Nevertheless, I am afraid that one clear and audible " damn " was heard in every department from lingerie to carpets when, on being told to play something suitable as a signal for the appearance of the bride's gown, our pianist absent-mindedly struck up the " Merry Widow." The following afternoon from 3.30 to six o'clock was spent in playing at the annual tea of a big laundry. It was a strange party, and no one appeared to derive any pleasure from it except ourselves and an over-dressed gentleman in a tail-coat and spongebag trousers who made a long and impassioned speech on the washing merits of Shephards' Shirts. Half an hour after " God Save the King " had closed down the laundry party, we were due at a coming-of-age dinner at the Dorchester. This consisted of eighty guests and so many toasts that before the dinner was three-quarters finished we had played " For He's a Jolly Good Fellow " no less than seventeen times. We ended the week at a dock-hands' " flannel dance " down at Grays in Essex. The dancers disliked both our playing and our appearance and made no bones about saying so at short intervals throughout the evening.

The hardest jobs of all were hunt or hospital balls. Country folk seem to possess greater stamina than Londoners. Certainly on the dance floor their staying-power is far more impressive. Very few London dances go on after 3 a.m., but in the country the guests still have ample strength at 4 a.m. to demand a reel or jig from an already wilting band, or—worse still—some deplorable country dance which generally lasts for a quarter of an hour, during which the same four bars of " olde worlde " music have to be played at least a hundred times. Undefeated even then, the pink-coated die-hards of the Shires insist on finishing off the night—and the band—with " D'you Ken John Peel," which must be accelerated *ad lib.* until every dancer is piled up in a heap in one corner of the room.

The softest job was a four weeks' engagement in the restaurant at Grosvenor House, where they paid us a most comfortable salary and only required us to play each night from 10.30 to eleven and again from 12.30 to one. The hour and a half's pause between the two sessions was spent in holding impromptu supper parties in the cabaret artists' dressing-room. Quite often, kind-hearted waiters augmented our nightly meal of scrambled eggs and beer with some of the dishes which their customers had neglected to finish !

During the five years in which the band flourished we learnt quite a lot about good—and bad— manners from our clients and their guests. Admittedly we were the only women's band to play at private dances in London, but surely there was nothing very remarkable about that ? Yet, judging from the nudging and staring that sometimes went on we might have been four exhibits at a freak show. An endless source of amusement was provided for us by certain of our contemporaries at whose parents' houses we had quite often dined in the days when we, too, had gone as guests to private dances. In our new professional capacity we were gloriously and deliberately cut by these humourless young women whenever they danced to our music.

(Let me say, here and now, that it is inadvisable to irritate a dance band unduly. They are capable of retaliating and spoiling your evening quite a lot, by playing a short number when you are dancing with an Adonis or an unending tango when you are hopping round the room with an eighty-year-old host. The " Paul Jones " or " Change Partners " dance is another grand opportunity for band mischief. Time and again, by a nicely judged halt in the music, we have forced two sworn enemies to dance together ; one unforgettable night we even managed to reunite a divorced couple for the space of a brief, icebergian rumba.)

The Winter Sports Season of 1931–32 will be remembered sadly by those unfortunates who, owing to a rise in patriotism and a fall in income, were obliged to forego Switzerland and take their skis and skates to Scotland. Under the circumstances Swiss hotel-keepers were chary of engaging dance bands, so we also went north and accepted a ten-weeks' contract at the Fife Arms Hotel, Braemar. Always treacherous and perverse, the Scottish climate excelled itself. It was the warmest winter that had been experienced for years. The sun shone, the birds sang and the flowers came out weeks before their time. Sometimes it rained gently but firmly and occasionally there were thunder and hailstorms, but the thermometer stayed at summer temperature and even the highest tops of the hills remained a virgin green. Unperturbed by any of these meteorological errors the majority of visitors were determined, at all costs, to preserve the Spirit of Switzerland in Scotland.

Regardless of the summerlike temperature they elected to walk about the muddy countryside dressed in the very thickest of ski-ing suits and boots, much to the gaping astonishment of the local inhabitants who rapidly became convinced that Braemar had been turned into a northern branch of Colney Hatch. Out of the ten weeks which we spent in that sad little village there were exactly three days on which it was just possible to ski. The excitement was terrific. Skis were waxed and rucksacks strapped on. More and more scarves and sweaters were donned as for a North Pole expedition. Press photographers and the Movietone News came north and drove madly round the countryside trying to get " shots " before all the snow had melted away. Two practically flat fields were turned into nursery slopes. Herr Schmidt, a ski-ing expert from St. Moritz whose opinion of Scotland does not bear repetition, was heard politely requesting fallen beginners not to lie too long as the heat of their bodies caused ominous green patches to appear through the precious snow. One of those mornings the banjo player and I decided to try a bit of luge-ing. Laboriously we climbed up a steep path above the golf course ; groaningly we extended ourselves, stomachs down, on two very small toboggans ; majestically we started down the hill at a comfortable twenty miles an hour. " What a lovely view," said I, and carelessly took my eyes off the track and admired the surrounding scenery. I shall never luge in Scotland again. While I wasn't looking, the snow came to an end, the toboggan stopped dead and I went on—face downwards where a cow had lately stood. . . .

Towards the close of 1932 we took a winter engagement out at Engelberg. "How lovely," said
envious friends who saw us and our thirty-four
pieces of luggage off from Victoria. "How over-
rated," said the saxophonist who found no beauty
in crossing the Lake of Lucerne after eighteen hours
travelling and four changes. "How unspeakable,"
said I, realising that the time had come at last when
I must put on skis. At Engelberg the nursery slopes
are just on the outskirts of the village. They are
steep and slippery and at the bottom is a monastery
wall of the most un-Christian hardness. With
something akin to the desperate courage of the
early martyrs I flattened myself out a hundred times
against that wall, while ski-ing monks with flapping
cloaks swooped serenely past like crows, and schools
of children squeaked and chattered and practised
perfect Telemarks and "Christie" turns. How I
loathed and detested the whole business. My nose
bled, and reports like pistol shots went off in my
ears the higher I climbed. Struggling uphill was
odious enough ; coming down again was nothing
short of a nightmare. One did not merely *fall*
every seven yards. One hurtled through space and
finished in positions qualified to drive any professional contortionist mad with envy. "Don't be
so helpless," angrily I was admonished as I lay with
one ski flat underneath me and the other twisted at
some extraordinary angle undiscovered by Euclid.
"Chuck your legs up in the air and the skis will
disentangle themselves. . . ." One sunny afternoon light dawned. The altogether detestable art

of ski-ing was utterly beyond me. It was no use striving any longer to attain what was, for me, a physical impossibility. Whereupon, slightly unbalanced by this joyous discovery, I sat suddenly and heavily down upon my left thumb and broke it, thereby making quite clear that I intended taking no further part in winter sports—either that season or at any future one.

The band has now gone out of existence. Marriage removed the banjo player, and quite suddenly and inexplicably, I was transplanted from jazz to journalism. Instead of sitting up all night I now have to sit down all day. To start working on the staff of a weekly review was a solemn and somewhat alarming experience after five irresponsible years of band-playing. Moreover, the high-brows of Bloomsbury are a very different proposition from the low-brows of Syncopation. Different and sad and unbending they seem—and considerably less worldly wise. " Hot music " producers *versus* " hot-air " merchants. . . . There is no vestige of culture or art in the make-up of a dance-band professional (six hours hard playing a night soon does away with any signs of " temperament "), but there is enough nonsense talked by the pseudo-musical " souls " of Bloomsbury to convince one that the " band boys " can more than hold their own when it comes to a sound all-round knowledge of harmony, technique and, in fact, music. I have never forgotten one after-dinner oration by a Bloomsbury-ite. His subject was " The Emotional Reaction to Beethoven." After two thousand verbal variations on a theme of " tripe " he proceeded to the piano and for twenty minutes massacred the "Appassionata" sonata to such an extent that it was practically unrecognisable.

Sometimes in the office I am taken very severely to task by the editor and assistant editor. "We are simply appalled by your ignorance," they groan. "You are completely uneducated." So I am. Doubtless I should have spent five years at college instead of in a dance band. What a lot of fun I should have missed.

The First Time I Rented a House

by

HUGH KINGSMILL

HOTELS at famous pleasure resorts open with
the beginning of the season and close with the end
of the season. Were Saint Moritz to return to St.
Moritz at the beginning of November, he would
find almost as little to distract his religious meditations as when, with austere satisfaction, he first
noted from beneath his cowl the bleakness of the
Upper Engadine. But in more modest pleasure
resorts there are generally two or three small hotels
which, though full only from June to September,
keep open throughout the year. In hotels of this
kind the dead months are a heavy drain on the proprietor, for he will probably have a family to support,
and will certainly have a couple of old retainers,
who are hardened to his ways, as he to theirs.
Then there is the drainage to be touched up, and
a coat of paint to be applied to the more conspicuous portions of the hotel, and, if there is a rival
hotel up the road, he may yield to a nervous impulse
to instal another bathroom. So he is glad of anyone
who will contribute, however meagrely, to his
expenses, and when Christmas comes round feels a
very genuine good-will towards any guests who have
not escaped with the rest.

On Christmas Day, 1930, the family Kingsmill
(my wife and myself, Tony aged seven, and the

baby Edmee) were made a great fuss of by Monsieur and Madame Charveron, owners of the Hotel Belle-Rive, Thonon-les-Bains, which is on the French shore of Lake Geneva. A special dinner, which we took with the Charverons, was cooked for us, a bottle of champagne was opened, and after dinner we danced to the wireless. On these rare festal occasions the pale harassed face of Madame Charveron used to relax into an expression of precarious almost girlish happiness. A native of South Germany, she would tremble between tears and smiles, and from time to time cast a tenderly reproachful glance at her solid French husband, who was and looked the cook of the establishment.

This dinner, without disrespect to the champagne, was the high-water mark of our popularity with the Charverons. By April, when the hotel was beginning to fill, they had cooled towards us, the rate we paid comparing unfavourably with what they charged guests who came only for two or three weeks ; and by June, when a series of mischances had put it out of my power to keep at all abreast with the monthly bill, they were decidedly irritable.

While waiting for news from my agent, David Higham, who was trying to place a book I had written in the winter, I started a series of parodies for the *English Review*, which my friend Douglas Jerrold promised to pay for as he received them. Dorothy and I were convinced that a book of parodies would sell, and I set to with enthusiasm. But I soon found that nothing is so slow and difficult to write as a parody, and my temper was not improved by the fact that nearly all the writers I was imitating were either dead and famous, or alive and best-sellers. Especially do I remember how when I was doing P. G. Wodehouse my laughter would turn to despair at the facility with which Bertie Wooster handed out tenners to Jeeves.

At the end of June Madame Charveron suggested that we should find rooms elsewhere, while continuing to have our meals at the hotel, so we took rooms in the Café de Navigation near by, which was the favourite pub of the fishermen of the village. Maurice, the shambling, vacant-eyed, but indefatigable porter of the Belle-Rive, said he would transport what we needed in a basket, and that Madame Charveron would store our trunks in the hotel. Annoyed at this attempt to deprive us of our trunks, Dorothy vetoed this suggestion, and Maurice, after smiling weakly at her for a few moments, agreed to take our trunks over when they were ready.

Situated on the fourth floor of the café, and lit by two large windows, our new room was a haven we left with reluctance for meals at the Belle-Rive and the glum visage of Madame Charveron. Through one window a group of poplars was visible whose leaves on fine mornings twinkled in the early breeze, and through the other window we looked across the lake to the Swiss shore, which in the clear air before a storm seemed only on the other side of a wide river, but on calm summer days receded into the hazy distance. As evening fell, points of light sprang out on the opposite shore, and as the darkness deepened the lights grew brighter and the slopes above them more obscure, till at last only a string of lights remained.

One day, perhaps feeling depressed by our low spirits, Tony went off for the afternoon. At six we were anxious. Seven, eight—our alarm became panic, we rung up the police station, and we inquired from the children in the fishing village if Tony had told them his plans for the afternoon. At last, after nine, we saw him padding down the hill. On his way through the fishing village, the children had warned him of our agitation, and as he came into view he looked like Macbeth, Act Five, when all that was within him did condemn itself for being there.

" Where have you been ? " I shouted. " What on earth have you been doing ? "

" I . . . I . . ."

" Yes ? "

" I . . ."

" Yes ? "

" I was looking at a p-pig."

As it was now the full season, the rent of our two rooms at the café was more than £6 a month, so when towards the end of July Dorothy heard that there was a furnished villa up the road with a very low rent, we hastened along to look at it.

Les Sapins, as it was called, was clearly a villa only by the courtesy of its owner. To a less partial eye it was a cottage which had not been white-washed for some time. A woodcut of it in a history of literature, with for title " Birthplace of Rousseau," would have had a pleasing old-world air, but as a concrete object in the modern world it was depressing, though in our anxiety to find something cheaper than the café we forced ourselves to agree that it might be worse.

The landlord, Monsieur Z., was an Italian who had a grocery in the town—a grim person, lean, dark, with angry brown eyes, and thin compressed lips. His wife, a very fat woman, seemed more amiable, but was perhaps only less forceful. During our first talk with Monsieur Z., he exerted himself to be charming, told us that during the war he had been a tailor in Paris, where he had met many English officers and learned to esteem the English character; and when I said I wrote, he spoke of his love of Dante, and confessed that he himself was a poet.

We went over the house with him. The ground floor consisted of a kitchen and sitting-room, the second floor of a bathroom and two bedrooms, and the rent he asked for an eleven months' tenancy was equivalent at that time to a little over £4 a month, which we thought most reasonable.

Undisturbed by Madame Charveron's prophecy that we would find Les Sapins very damp in the winter, we moved in at once. A faint feeling of pride at being for the first time in my life the tenant of a complete house soon faded as the drawbacks of the house began to reveal themselves. It was really a gardener's cottage on the property of Monsieur Z., who had a genuine villa about fifty yards up the slope at the bottom of which Les Sapins lay. Trees overshadowed us from three sides, and the front door opened straight on to the main road, along which during the season there rushed a stream of cars whose noise was deepened into a hollow roar by a stone wall opposite. Within, the house was gloomy and hard to clean, but Dorothy, who knew something about interior decoration, stripped the walls of the dirty paper and applied a coat of cream paint and stained and wax polished the floors. As we had the greatest difficulty in extracting bed linen and cooking utensils from Monsieur Z., we had to fill the gaps with purchases in the town, and the thought of the creditors I was amassing frequently came between me and my attempts to imitate the styles of Dr. Johnson, H. G. Wells and Oscar Wilde.

As the motor cars dwindled and before the cold set in Les Sapins was bearable, though Dorothy, after making the interior as attractive as it could be made short of pulling the house down and rebuilding it, was greatly distressed one October afternoon to discover that Monsieur Z. had that morning caused the west wall of Les Sapins to be plastered with a vast advertisement of Olio Sasso, an Italian product of which he was the sole agent in Thonon. I rushed up to his shop, but was more angry than effective, and Dorothy did not congratulate me on the indemnity I wrung from him, namely, the cancellation of our water rate—fifteen francs a month.

It was when the frost set in in December and we began to have trouble with burst pipes that our real trials with the house began. By the third week in February we could stand its manifold torments no longer, and calling on Monsieur Z., told him that we were leaving at the end of February. I had had so many rows with him by this date that as soon as he saw me he exclaimed that he would not listen to what I had to say, so we went on to the local bailiff to inquire if, in all the circumstances, which I explained in detail, I was legally entitled to leave at the end of February and refuse to pay the 2,000 francs due on the balance of my tenancy. The bailiff, a round-faced, bouncing little man with quick blue eyes, looked thoughtful, scratched the side of his nose, and then, his face lighting up, leaned confidentially forward. " I will tell you what to do, Monsieur. Give me the two thousand francs. Then, when Monsieur Z. begins a process, I shall pay the two thousand francs into court. Thus the judge will understand that you are serious."

" And after he has understood that I am serious ? "

The bailiff made a gesture which seemed to disclaim any further insight into the minds of judges.

" I haven't got two thousand francs," I said. His face darkened and he drew back from me. I pressed him for a definite opinion whether I could leave Les Sapins at the end of the month for another house in Thonon, at the same time sending my new address to Monsieur Z. with a statement of my complaints, and he said I was entitled to take this step. The next day I called on him again, and he drafted a letter for me, but his account of our experiences at Les Sapins was miserably brief and perfunctory. It was a theme which would have taxed even the powers of Monsieur Z.'s favourite poet, and when I showed the bailiff's scribble to Dorothy, she suggested that we should draw up our own account. So we sat down and composed the following letter, dating it from the last day of February, for it was our intention to send it from our new home.

Monsieur,

I am sending you this registered letter to confirm the statement made to you at your shop by myself and my wife on February 17th, that we were leaving Les Sapins at the end of February. We came to discuss the situation with you, but you refused to listen, and displayed your usual lack of courtesy.

Our experiences with the bathroom, culminating on February 16th, are our chief source of dissatisfaction. As soon as the frost began in December we asked for instructions for avoiding burst pipes. You told us that it was necessary only to leave the tap in the kitchen running. This we did, but nevertheless, all the pipes in the bathroom froze, and we were unable to use the bathroom for more than a week. As soon as the weather became warmer, one of the bathroom pipes burst and the water came through the ceiling. When the domestic asked you to turn off the water you were rude to her and refused to concern yourself with the matter. My wife informed me of your refusal, I visited you, and it was only after an unpleasant dispute that you agreed to have the pipe repaired. We were forty-eight hours without water. After the pipe was repaired we found that the geyser would no longer work, and we have not been able to use it since December, but preferred this discomfort rather than have another dispute with you.

You asked us in the event of another frost to keep the bathroom taps running as well as the kitchen tap. When the frost set in in February, we turned on the kitchen tap, the bathroom taps and the tap by the garden door, in spite of the vexatious noise caused thereby. Nevertheless, when the thaw arrived, the pipe burst again and flooded the whole of the ground floor. I went up to see you and you informed me for the first time that the bathroom was not to be used in winter, and you accused us of not carrying out your instructions about leaving the taps running. My wife, myself and the domestic were an hour getting the water out of the house, and our trunks and the overcoats and hats in the entrance hall were all damaged.

This experience, coming on top of a long succession of annoyances, decided us to leave Les Sapins. Before we entered the house you promised to supply us with all the necessaries customary when a house is taken furnished. A few days after we entered you demanded back the bed linen, and when we asked for kitchen utensils to replace the broken ones you gave us, you sent down two small saucepans. Later when we asked for blankets you gave us only two small ones. We therefore provided our own linen, blankets and most of the kitchen utensils. We have now been informed that we ought to have insisted on your supplying all these things, and that the sum of five hundred francs a month is exorbitant for the little you have supplied.

In October you disfigured the west wall of Les Sapins with an enormous advertisement of Olio Sasso without asking our permission. As soon as the winter began we discovered how damp the house was. We have spent four hundred francs a month on coal to warm it, which has only resulted in filling the place with vapour and increased the dripping of water on the walls. The constant humidity has given my wife and the domestic rheumatism, and myself sciatica, and the doctor has had to attend all three. The electric lights are constantly fusing, and the chairs are constantly coming unstuck, both of which are due, the workmen have told us, to humidity. We were warned of this humidity before we took the house. We asked you if these rumours were true, and we accepted your word that they were not.

We have done all in our power to make a success of your house, having spent fifteen hundred francs in furnishing the bathroom with linoleum and a bidet, re-papering and repainting the house, waxing the floors and putting up shelves in the kitchen, and engaging an extra domestic simply to keep the house clean. But our patience has been exhausted by all the annoyances enumerated and your constant discourtesy and refusal to accept your obligations.

A Lizard the Size of a Young Alligator——

I enclose five hundred francs for our rent up to the end of February. I also enclose the keys. We have left the house thoroughly cleaned and have not removed any of the fixtures we have supplied. As you have not fulfilled your obligations as the landlord, I am terminating my tenancy with the above payment.

Hugh Kingsmill Lunn.

The next day we were taken by a house agent to a delightful little house on the tableland of Thonon, 200 feet above the lake. The view was open in all directions, extending southwards over miles of uplands to the conical peak of Dent d'Oche, and to the east, north and west, embracing more than half the Lake of Geneva and the long line of the Jura beyond. The house was called " *Rien et Tout,*" and I was curious to hear how the agent would explain this somewhat Barriesque name. My question greatly embarrassed him, for I put it to him before signing the contract, and he was naturally reluctant to explain that the " *Rien* " was the material value of the place, and the " *Tout* " its spiritual value. " *Ça veut dire . . .*" he contorted his hands. " *C'est difficile à expliquer . . .*" he twisted his eyebrows. " *Rien—ça exprime. . . .*" I patted him on the shoulder and he smiled wanly back.

On our last day at Les Sapins a lizard, the size of a youngish alligator, darted across the sitting-room floor into the kitchen, where our maid swiped it over the head with the poker. " *C'est mort,*" she called out triumphantly, but we told her she need

not bring in the corpse. Our nerves were on edge
with the thought of the next day, and I speculated
in silence on what might rain upon us if one of the
mildewed walls fell in.

The following morning a cart came for our luggage, which the two carriers had just piled upon it
when Monsieur Z. rushed up with an order from
our friend the bailiff that we were to put our luggage
back in Les Sapins, and appear before him at
eleven. While the carriers, with provoking un-
concern, were returning our effects into the house,
our maid came out with the baby in the pram.
Monsieur Z., whom his wife had now joined, tried
to stop the maid, and a duel of abuse broke out
between me on the one side and Monsieur and
Madame Z. on the other, in the course of which the
maid and Edmee disappeared in the direction of
our new home. Dorothy and I went back into the
house, and there, surrounded by our trunks, we
waited until it was time to go up to the bailiff.
He greeted us coldly, informed us that Monsieur
Z.'s lawyer wished to see us, and gave us the address.
As we were leaving, Dorothy asked him in a voice
some degrees colder than his own why he had told
me I was entitled to do something he had just
prevented me from doing. He blinked, but said
nothing. In great gloom we made our way to
Monsieur Z.'s lawyer, who to our surprise greeted
us in a friendly way—a stout comfortable little
man to whom our hearts warmed at once. We
handed him our letter in its French translation ;
he read it slowly, and then asked me if I had any
proposal to make. I said that I would pay a

thousand francs in a post-dated cheque, but would not pay the full rent unless ordered to by the court. He asked us to return in two hours. When we came back we found Monsieur and Madame Z. with the lawyer. Holding up the letter with a solemn expression, the lawyer said : " This statement has clearly been drawn up by a lawyer. Monsieur Z., I advise you to accept the offer this gentleman has made." Monsieur Z. put up a great show of resistance, though he clearly felt that two months' rent in addition to the improvements we had made at Les Sapins was more than any court would have given him. At last, after I had agreed to pay the costs of our dispute, 150 francs, he yielded.

" *J'ai perdu mille francs,*" he groaned.

" *Vous avez un bon bidet pour ça,*" I replied, and he smiled for the first time since I had signed the lease, and said that that was a characteristically English remark.

We returned to Les Sapins with Madame Z., now very garrulous, and she and Dorothy checked the inventory while the carriers piled the luggage on the cart again. On top of the trunks a long plain deal bookcase, which Dorothy had had made to order and which had been secured to the sitting-room wall by nails, rested precariously. The cart crawled off, the bookcase waggling on top, and we followed it towards the west and the setting sun as in the tranquil ending of a film, Dorothy leaning on my arm in great fatigue, for the birth of our youngest child, whom we used to refer to as " Huglun," the favourite spelling of my name among the Thonon tradesmen, was only a few weeks ahead.

At the door of " *Rien et Tout* " we were met by the landlady with bowls of steaming soup. Tony had not yet arrived from school. We had given him detailed instructions how to find our new house, but seemingly he had forgotten them, and we were beginning to get anxious when he turned up in the custody of a benevolent stranger, in time to finish the soup.

The First Time I did This and That

by

ROSE MACAULAY

THE FIRST TIME I DID THIS
AND THAT

STOLE FROM A SHOP

To prevent misunderstanding, let me hasten to add that the first time has been (so far) also the last. There is obviously a living to be made out of this career, but I do not think that I am intelligent enough to make it. Even that first time, long ago, I am now inclined to think that my act was not unperceived by the kindly owner whom I robbed.

It was one of those dark, low-roofed shops, smelling pleasantly of wine, vegetables, macaroni and dust, where stores of twisted spaghetti, maize, beans and other dry vegetables stood about the uneven stone floor in sacks. It was dim and cool after the hot street ; sunshine slanted in through the open door, and in it the dust and flour danced. My father was talking to the shopkeeper, paying a bill, purchasing commestibles, I forget what. I and some brothers and sisters were with him ; I suppose we had turned in on our way, going for a walk. I stood beside a large sack full of beans. Lovely beans, hard, pale in colour, and freckled with spots of divers colours—blue, green, brown, pink, purple, like an Easter egg. It was these speckles that made them lovely and desirable in my eyes, like thrushes' eggs in a nest, like little trout in a brook. I coveted them. I did a dreadful, a tremendous, thing ; I put out a stealthy hand and took one, slipping it into the pocket of my frock.

Until the deed was done, I had not realised across what gulf I stepped. But, as we left the *drogheria*, I knew myself on the further side of that line which divided thieves from those who are not thieves. I had stolen from a shop : I was a bean stealer, a faboklept. I had entered the unholy company of robbers. Of course, I had long ere this stolen domestically : once a biscuit, once half a strawberry (overcome with remorse, I had replaced the other half on the dish), once jam from a pot. But domestic robbery was different ; one could not be imprisoned for it. I was now a common criminal.

Still, there lay the speckled bean in my pocket, rattling against my knife. I could not show it to any one, but I possessed it. It was a lovely bean.

WROTE A NOVEL

" Wrote " is wrong ; the pencil was wielded by one of my sisters, whose superior age gave her more power over it. The novel was a collaboration ; we lay together under the nursery table, out of the way of the trampling feet of others less literarily minded, and composed it between us. It was called " Gish and Gee," and it was illustrated. It was a narrative of the strange adventures which befell our two heroines, young persons of lawless minds and that infinite capacity for encountering and surviving disasters which characterises the heroes and heroines of all thrillers. What the

224

Miss Macaulay did not Write Her First Novel because She could not Write. Fortunately Her Elder Sister Collaborated with Her.

adventures were I do not now remember ; what I do remember is the joy and excitement of the creator, the thrill and throb of the imagination at work, the transportation of the spirit from mundane life to the worlds of mystic fervour where the artist treads on air.

It was not long after this that I began to write stories and poems on my own account. It was the beginning of a long career as author ; a career which I now see should never have included the composition of narrative fiction. For I have ever been the most incompetent, the least efficient, of novelists ; I cannot think up a good story, or write its middle, though I can only too easily manage the end. I feel sure that Gish and Gee were ill-drawn characters ; their story had no moral and no sequence, their adventures no plausibility. It was, in fact, a work of pure imagination, more akin to the epic or saga than to the novel.

I miss Gish and Gee. I have often thought that they are the protagonists I require for my novels to-day. What I want is some impersonal adventurer, who shall rove through sea and land, through tropical forest and island scenery, dive into lagoons among the coral and the fish, without concern for personal relationships, reality, or plot. What I want is a mere excuse for writing down words, a peg on which to hang phrases, style, rhythm, language, imagery, ideas. Poetry or prose, it matters little ; but I would that I could return to that infant firmness which absolved Gish and Gee from the necessity of endeavouring to be real and plausible little girls. Alas, incompetent that I am, I early took a wrong turning (so far as prose was concerned) and tried, all in vain and all bewildered, to write about life. Bewildered, because Life will not really go into words ; besides, I want words for other purposes.

But Gish and Gee are gone into the shadows : I can only with difficulty recall those round, blank faces and triangular bodies which represented them, so fitly, on our drawing paper.

SAW MYSELF IN PRINT

This did not occur until I was fifteen (unless I am to count the effusions which we set up for ourselves with our family printing press). It was, to be sure, only in a school magazine. But I had done more than describe a hockey match or a ramble : I had written a poem. A prize had been offered for the best poem about the sea, and I had won it. It was, I remember, a thoroughly bad poem. I had known that it was bad, but until I saw it in print, in those magic little black letters which bestow the prestige of real literature, I had not known how bad, or how embarrassing it would be to have those feeble lines on the ocean exposed to the view of my peers. I had, I thought, written very many much better poems in the course of my poetic career, which had begun early. But it was not considered good form in my family to make public our compositions (except those intended for the various family magazines that, from time to time, ran for a few enthusiastic weeks and then perished, in the approved manner of periodicals). Our private compositions we kept private. So I alone had seen my verses, which, a luxuriant and ill-pruned growth, had, since a tender age, filled many exercise books. No doubt that most were as bad as this that was printed. My ardent and callow emotions on regarding the beauties of nature, my dreams of heroic adventure, my tragic *weltschmerzen*, all found expression in swinging rhythms and tripping lines, or in the unshackled ease of the irregular Pindaric ode (which I thought I composed particularly well), but fortunately none had seen what is called the light of day, until these crude and shaming stanzas about the ocean, which I had sent in an hour of vain folly and now saw dishonouring me all over a page. I consoled myself by reflecting that they had won a prize, so had presumably by the adjudicators been found less bad than the other entries. And what, after all, is print, that we should regard it as either honouring or dishonouring us? May one not have such thoughts, such emotions, as one pleases, and express them in such ways as one chooses, even if in print, without being scorned and reprehended by those who have the impertinence to read what one has written? Let readers, critics and reviewers mind their own business, I say.

Still, I was definitely embarrassed. How many times I was to be similarly embarrassed in later life, I did not then reflect.

SHOT A BIRD

I was fourteen. In the garden and field of an uncle, an uncle so kind and so ill-judged that he would invite us to spend our summer holidays with him, we prowled with our catapults, shooting pebbles at trees, at cows (who appeared almost as little moved by them as did the trees) and at any other objects which invited our attention. When I shot the bird, I was in the garden, with two brothers. It was a green bird : I think a greenfinch, and it was in a tree. My brothers directed my attention to it ; I suppose that I had, for the moment, the best catapult, or possibly the only one we had out with us. Anyhow, it occurred that I was the person to aim at the green bird. I cannot now look back clearly into the mind of the child who took that aim ; it is certain that I never visualised the bird as shot. By some fluke, I aimed straight, and hit it ; it fell to the ground. We ran up to it. It was dead. My brothers were exultant and delighted. They had the sportsman's instinct. There sprang wide between us the gulf of sex, for I turned away in tears. I had slain a bird ; that little singing, flying, bustling, jubilant creature would sing, fly, exult, bustle no more. I had put a stop to all that ; I had, on a chance whim, pulled a piece of elastic and murdered the innocent gay life which had done me no harm, but only asked to be allowed to enjoy itself in the garden as I did myself.

For weeks I was haunted by that small plumy corpse ; I still am so.

REALISED THE INACCURACY OF ADULTS

It was the eve of my fourth birthday. I had retired to bed, my mind, as was natural, obsessed with the great morrow that was to dawn. A nurse and a nursery maid were conversing together in the room. I said to them, speaking my thoughts from a full heart, " To-morrow I shall be four." They, or one of them, returned, " Four's nothing." I was not offended, or hurt ; I was merely uncomprehending. I tried to put them right. I said, " It's not nothing ; it's something. It's four." They replied again, " Four's nothing." A tiresomely eristic child, I attempted to argue this assertion that $4 = 0$, but they did not heed ; they continued their conversation with one another about something else, leaving me weakly but stubbornly protesting against what even I knew to be an error in arithmetic. I did not realise until much later that these women had been using the figure known as hyperbole ; that " nothing " in their mouths meant " very little." I do not know why I had been so unobservant an infant as not to have perceived long before this that adults were addicted to this figure ; I suppose that I had a higher linguistic standard for grown people than for my own generation, who talked freely, as I knew, of trees and animals being " miles high," of the things we carried weighing " tons," of ourselves, when warm, being " boiling." But, for some reason, I did not understand that my nurse and nursery-maid were using a similar figure ; I was merely bewildered by their numerically inaccurate statement. I already knew them as not being well informed about the facts of life, for when I asked them the size of a new-born Esquimaux baby, they did not tell me, but said " Why ? " And now I knew them to be quite untruthful as well, trying to persuade me that the number four was not something but nothing. Tiresome little precisian that I was, the last waking moments of my fourth year were moments of bewilderment.

WENT TO SCHOOL

Through a door in a pink wall we trooped, the little Italian girls from the town, the three little English new girls from the Villa Inglese, whose parents had suddenly decided to send them daily for a while to the convent school of Santa Caterina. Rather strange we felt, very *inglese*, very, in brief, odd. We had straw hats to remove ; our fellow-scholars were mostly hatless or handkerchiefed. At the end of the prayers which opened school, the little *inglesi* were bidden to remain seated during a prayer for their conversion to the true Church, for the *inglesi* were little heretics. This was definitely embarrassing ; the *inglesi* endeavoured to look as though they did not understand what was occurring, but looked, in fact, self-conscious. Afterwards (or was it another morning ?) one of the nuns remarked to us that in England, no doubt, people did not go to church. My eldest sister, a child of spirit and patriotism, replied that, on the contrary, in England the population made a habit of attending church every day. The good nuns were surprised and impressed, and the *inglesi* felt that they had kept the Union Jack flying.

The nuns who taught us were kind and rather charming. Suor Commassina, our chief instructress, resembled, and knew it, a picture of the Madonna that hung in the classroom ; she would purse her mouth and turn up her eyes and cross her hands before her, in the most saintly manner imaginable.

Another, whose name now eludes me, had a less celestial air, seemed more of this world. They all taught us Genoese French in Genoese Italian ; they all suspected their pupils of holding communication through the classroom windows with men in the street below, and, when the school procession passed a man on a walk, bade it lower its eyes. English schoolmistresses behaving thus would be revolting ; these Italian nuns were somehow charmingly endearing. So were most of their pupils.

We did not for long attend that school ; only, I think, through one spring and summer. Looking back, I remember most clearly the buzzing of flies in a hot classroom, pencils taking down Italian dictation slipping in hot fingers, Suor Commassina's rosy Madonna face turned reproachfully on ill-behaved scholars, the droning, nasal chant of voices from the infant school reciting whatever it is that the infants of all races seem perpetually to recite, and the hot glare of the white dust on the stretch of road beyond the deep, shut-in streets of the town, whereon we walked home at noon.

FELL IN LOVE

It was probably not the first time, since infants, we are told, love with all the extremes of passion and abandon from the very first. I have no doubt that I fell in love with my mother, my father, my nurse, and all the other appropriate objects of juvenile passion. But the first time that I remember experiencing this so exciting and disturbing emotion was when I must have been, I think, four years old, and my mother read *Ivanhoe* aloud to us.

Wilfred of Ivanhoe had every qualification for an inspirer of a grand passion. He was a knight ; he had courage and courtesy ; he was always in the right place in the nick of time to rescue the emperilled ; he pitted his wits and his sword successfully against the villainous Brian de Bwoggilber ; he rode on to the tourney field in disguise, as the Black Knight, and performed prodigies of valour and skill amid general acclamation. He was, in short, an excessively perfect gentle knight, and the inevitable lode-star of infantile adoration. In my family, he became a divinity. I thrilled at his entries, his gallant words, his noble deeds. I lay awake in my cot and thought of him. When my mother played the piano, he seemed to be riding by, glorious as an army with banners, and I, his young page, rode behind on a milk-white pony with a long black tail, ready to rush in with sword and javelin to defend him from the foe (de Bwoggilber) should he be unhorsed. I saw myself standing over him with raised sword, keeping the enemy at bay until he struggled to his feet. He did not forget this service ; he dubbed me knight for it after the fight, tapping my shoulder with his sword and saying, " Rise, Sir Richard " (for Richard was usually, in my dreams, my name). When we had tournaments, we had to be Ivanhoe and the wicked Knight Templar in turns. We called one of our dolls by the hallowed name, and noble feats that sawdust being performed ; but I was not entirely comfortable about this dragging a hero about by a rag arm, throwing him down banks and into strange undignified predicaments ; once his head came off, and once we left him out in the garden all night in the rain.

First love : how giddy, how inebriant a passion ! How it filled the sounding air with trumpets and with tabers, with the fluttering of pennants and the shivering of lances, with all the heady music of the spheres ! Other loves were to follow, in hot and crowded succession ; Richard, the little Duke of Normandy, and Osmond his brave squire ; Sir Kenneth in the *Talisman ;* Jason, Theseus, the Black Prince, Richard Cœur de Lion, Sir Guy Morville, Hugo Wharncliffe, a hundred more noble and adventurous beings. For mine was a most passionate and enamoured youth. I do not say that I never again loved anyone so greatly as I loved Wilfred of Ivanhoe ; but I am almost certain that I never loved anyone more. If throbbing heart and labouring breast be the signs, prickling skin and quivering lip, transfigured world and enchanted musings, then I doted, devoutly doted, doted in idolatry, upon this spotless and most valiant man.

I should like to feel so again. Or would it be too disturbing ?

The First Time I did the " Goose-Step "

by

PRINCE   LEOPOLD   LOEWENSTEIN-WERTHEIM

WHEN I first did the Goose-Step I was thirteen years of age.

For all those readers who do not know what the goose-step is or who, having seen it only on the news reel in the cinema, think it is nothing but a rather odd way of marching, I offer the following interpretation :—

The goose-step is more than a way of marching : it is an elaborate system of mortification of the spirit—a kind of perverted Yoga, calculated to reduce men's great diversity of faculties to the one only, to obey. So that he may, in the case of war, move across the battlefield with the same mathematical precision with which at G.H.Q.'s the generals of the staff move their little flags over the map to indicate the goal of their strategical plans.

But even more than that : the goose-step is a ritual. It is the sacramental act of German militarism. It is the supreme consummation of the sergeant-major's " Weltenschauung " initiated by Prussia's first kings and passed on from generation to generation as a sacred trust.

When Germany was defeated in 1918, and began to remember her mission as a guardian of a great cultural heritage, we all hoped that she had broken with the goose-step and its odious mentality. But, alas, this proved to be a fallacy.

In 1935 the sergeant-major has again conquered the German nation. Hitler, the sergeant-major triumphant! In his movement the spirit of the goose-step has come to life again in all its drab splendour.

Hitler and I were practising the goose-step at the same time. That was in 1916, when I was thirteen years old. Hitler goose-stepped on the Western Front and I goose-stepped in the court-yard of the Royal Cadet Corps at Munich. Hitler loved the goose-step. I know I hated it. He now rules over a nation of 70 million people. Was I wrong in hating the goose-step? The reader will have to judge.

It was a beautiful sunny September day when my father and I walked along the streets of Munich. It was the day on which I entered the Cadet School. We did not speak much. My father asked me:

" Are you pleased ? "

And I answered : " Yes, Papa."

He always expected me to reply to his questions in a short manner and precisely to the point. This seemed to be even more indicated now that there was war, and one had little time to dwell on the emotional aspect of things.

" Only the civilian ' talks '," my father used to say. " A soldier repeats orders given to him and otherwise remains silent."

As I walked beside my father I admired him and, as I admired him, I despised myself.

" Walk on my right side," said my father, " for you keep on stumbling over my sword."

His sword had always exercised an almost magic spell on me. Its blade was delicately incised with inscriptions bearing testimony of the chivalry of the Uhlan regiment to which he belonged. It had a gilded basket and the top of the hilt represented a lion's head, inlaid with rubies.

Whenever my father referred to it he said :

" Your grandfather carried it at the proclamation of the Empire at Versailles, and one day you will carry it ! "

My father's sword slightly scraped the pavement, the silver spurs of his patent leather shoes tinkled like bells. My father wore a peace-time uniform, long green tunic, very narrow green trousers with broad cherry-red stripes. It was a beautiful uniform.

I looked at him and then at myself and the feeling overcame me that I looked ridiculous.

I wore a suit of crome yellow " Loden " with green lapels, a green waistcoat with silver buttons. I had knee-breeches, and the lower part of my legs were encased in thick, green woollen stockings. My shoes were of the pattern used for mountaineering, heavily nailed, the heels strengthened by a kind of iron horseshoe. I felt uncomfortable in my clothes ; the stockings caused an almost unbearable sensation of itching which radiated over my entire body. The garters holding these stockings in place were too tight. I was convinced that they obstructed the blood circulation and were responsible for the pallor of my face.

My father was sunburnt and of youthful appearance.

" Would I ever resemble him," I thought, " if only I wore a uniform ? "

To get rid of these absurd civilian clothes seemed to me the most essential thing at the moment. To get rid also of this ridiculous Tyrolese hat with its " Gamsbart," held by a brooch on which was inscribed " Gott strafe England."

My father, when saluting, nonchalantly lifted two fingers to the shiny shield of his cap. I always had to take off my hat, only to put it on again each time in what seemed to my father an entirely wrong fashion. He wanted me to wear my hat well on the forehead, whereas I thought it more tolerable to wear it on the back of my head. This always led to the same conversation :

" How often am I to tell you that one does not wear one's hat on one's neck but on one's forehead ? "

" Yes, Papa."

" I wish you would do as I tell you and remember, once and for all, to wear your hat like a young nobleman and not like a Jew in a synagogue."

" Yes, Papa."

The Cadet School was situated at a considerable distance from the centre of the town. The red brick building stood in a quiet square, looking very much like a London square, with a lawn and trees in the centre.

Along the frontage of the school the road was of asphalt especially suited for parading, as the asphalt provides good resonance, thus increasing in effect the rhythm of goose-stepping legs.

It was about three o'clock in the afternoon when my father and I reached the square. The sun sparkled on the shiny asphalt and but for a few boys roller-skating in front of the Cadet Corps (this should be forbidden, my father said), there was perfect stillness everywhere.

The term had not begun yet, but it had been my father's wish that I should enter one day earlier so that he could introduce me personally to the officers.

" I want to shake hands with these gentlemen of the infantry," my father said ; " they always feel honoured if one " (meaning the cavalry) " does, and this will be good for you."

As we entered the gates of the building, my father remarked, pointing at the Royal Bavarian Arms above :

" You know, of course, that these are our own arms and that you will be the only cadet to have his own coat of arms on his helmet."

" Yes, Papa."

I was very impressed.

The underclothing of the soldier is chosen by a standard quite different from the one of a bride-to-be. It is not meant to be seen and to arouse pleasant expectations. It is just an intermediary stage between the non-soldier and the fully dressed soldier. No one wants to undress a soldier, least of all the military administration which dresses him. Only a soldier in uniform is a soldier of whom the Father-land is proud, the girls jealous and the enemy afraid. In short, the undressed soldier is no soldier ; for all the use he is without his uniform he might be stuffed with sawdust. That is why the underclothing is of a strictly objective sobriety.

Six pairs of long pants of the coarsest material and with no shape whatever, with ribbons at the end to be tied round the ankles, six equally coarse shirts without collars, six night-shirts ditto, six pairs of cotton socks, were handed to me by the company sergeant-major.

" You should receive everything that is necessary complete at the school," my father had informed me ; " and if you are really in need of anything— I don't suppose you will be—write to me."

My first wish would have been to have different things altogether, the shirts and all the rest feeling damp, intolerably stiff and uncomfortable.

The company sergeant-major; a stout little man, who took charge of me when my father left me, seemed friendly disposed towards me. My father had given him a box of cigars.

*" Follow me," he said, " Cadet . . .? What is your name ? "

" Loewenstein."

" Loewenstein. Follow me, Cadet Loewenstein, we are going to fit you out beautifully."

He took me into the uniform depôt where hundreds of uniforms hung in rows. He cast a glance over my rather fragile figure and at random picked out a tunic.

" This will fit you."

It didn't in the least. It was much too wide.

" And a nice pair of trousers to match."

They were much too long.

" Trousers must be long," he explained. " They must touch the ground."

244

As I had never worn long trousers before I was unable to form any opinion except that they seemed too long even for long trousers.

I received in all :

One tunic and trousers for daily use.

One tunic and trousers for Sunday, church and special occasions.

One blouse to be worn during school hours.

One special drill suit of coarse, white linen.

Two overcoats.

Two caps and a helmet which the sergeant-major put on my head with the words :

" Now, Cadet . . . What is your name ? "

" Loewenstein."

" Cadet Loewenstein, you look really elegant."

He then gave me a belt, a bayonet, boots, material for cleaning buttons, soap, a tooth brush, once more asked me my name and dismissed me.

Loaded with my soldierly outfit, I walked back along the corridor to the dormitory that had been assigned to me. There I sat down on a hard narrow bed wondering what to do next. I looked around the dormitory which was a bleak room. Rows of beds, divided by small wardrobes, stood along the walls, rows of wash-stands in the middle of the room flanked by rows of huge shiny watercans. Everything in the room was arranged in straight lines, a picture of efficient desolation. Not that I saw it then as such, I had to accept everything as it was, and if watercans stood in straight rows it was probably because this was the best way for them to stand.

What puzzled me, however, was that the sergeant-major had asked me my name so often. It had never occurred to me that anybody should not know it, that I should ever come into contact with people whom I had to tell who I was. If he had asked me my Christian name, I would have understood, for it formed part of the concept " I " as I thought of myself; but my family name, that was something concerning my father alone, and whoever knew him also knew me.

After having waited for a while for something to happen, I concluded that no special preparations had been made to receive me and that the best thing I could do for the moment was to put on my uniform.

It took me quite a time to do so, but when I finally managed to hook the collar and to buckle the belt I looked at myself in the mirror and thought that I looked quite well, " better than in my civilian clothes, to say the least."

I then began to practise the salute as I had been used to see my father do it, lifting two fingers to the shield of the cap while slightly, almost imperceptibly, inclining the head forward. This I also seemed to be able to do quite well. I smiled into the looking-glass and addressed myself :

" Herr Lieutenant."

Suddenly I heard a sharp voice calling from the door :

" Cadet," and I turned round to see a young officer standing before me.

" Your name ? "

" Loewenstein."

" Thank you ! "

He left me.

This officer looked to me quite different from my father. He looked less decorative but more effective, more instrumental for war than my father.

His uniform was grey and devoid of anything that could have conveyed a meaning beyond the obvious one of being a professional attire for daily use. My father's uniform, on the contrary, seemed entirely detached from any immediate purpose. It seemed to live a purely symbolic life, hovering between the past and the future, a future, however, that appeared merely as a repetition of the past, a future that reduced the present to the *rôle* of a spectator in the continuous, timeless pageant of tradition.

My father in uniform was just a link in the chain of ancestral pictures that covered the walls of the castle, where I had lived as a child. There, twenty yards of corridor comprised twenty generations of ancestors, and according to where one chose to stand in the corridor these ancestors would recede into the past or become distant future.

This applied also to my father's portrait and would in time also apply to my own, and that was why I always looked upon my father's uniform as an expression of individualised tradition and had never thought that any practical purpose could be attached to a uniform.

While on that account the sight of Lieutenant Koch (that was the name of the young officer) in his field-grey uniform destroyed one illusion, his brisk manner contributed to strengthen another. There existed a poem by my father which began :

"The lieutenant is the bravest soldier in the
army . . ."

247

My father had resigned the army many years before the War as a lieutenant. With the outbreak of the War he had enlisted again and had been promoted lieutenant-colonel. He used to write poems of a most flaming patriotic kind with which we were highly edified and which we considered to be the result of a particularly deep insight into and special knowledge of the essence of all things.

At the time when I entered the Cadet School I made it my special duty to read my father's poems, so to speak, as a spiritual preparation for the career destined for me. The poem of the brave lieutenant had been revised in a second edition which was identical with the first save for one word; instead of " The lieutenant is the bravest soldier, etc.," it now read " The lieutenant-colonel."

Yet for me it remained the " lieutenant," because " lieutenant-colonel " broke the cadence of the rhyme, and this is the reason why henceforth Lieutenant Koch appeared to me as the very incarnation of bravery and military " virtus." (In his civilian life he was an insurance agent, which I learned many years after the War when he called on me suggesting I should take out a life insurance policy.)

During the weeks at the Cadet School I lived in a state of constant bewilderment, always trying to do the right thing in everything and never being able to find out what the right thing was. I did not then know that what makes a good soldier is the art of combining the knowledge of what is the right thing to do with the skill of never doing it. Until one has penetrated the mystery of this dual principle, on which rests what is commonly termed *esprit de corps*, one cannot feel at ease in the community of soldiers.

In an institution like the Cadet School with its century-old tradition, the *esprit de corps* was particularly strongly developed and its code demanded above all that life for the newcomer should be made as unpleasant as possible.

" Only when you really detest the military service will you begin to be a good soldier," we were told, " because," continued the argument, " only then will you fully realise what a despicable thing the civilian life is." (" Which "—this was, I suppose, the silent implication— " one cannot even detest and therefore also not love.")

So far as I was concerned I did detest the military service practically the whole time that it lasted, I only loved it at very rare moments.

We were taught the fundamentals of soldiering by being informed that a civilian can neither stand, nor walk, nor talk properly, in short, that he was altogether a being unfit for life and at his best a piece of raw material to be transformed into a man through the genius of the sergeant-major.

We were taught that the really important thing in standing was to have the tip of one's feet apart, at an angle of 45 degrees ; to have one's hands glued to the outer side of one's trousers, the middle finger in line with the seam ; to have one's chin and stomach pulled in and one's chest sticking out.

" You don't stand for your pleasure, you stand because you are a soldier."

We were taught that one could only walk decently

by swinging one's arms, the elbows pointing outwards, so that one's hands rhythmically reached the buckle of the belt. The instruction for the salute ran as follows :

" The salute begins when the *inferior* finds himself at a distance of six paces from the *superior*, and ends when the *inferior* has passed the *superior* by six paces. At six paces from the *superior*, the *inferior*, with a brisk movement, throws his head in the direction of the *superior*, at the same time lifting his right forearm to the level of his eyes (the upper arm forming an angle of 90 degrees to the spinal column), and touches the shield of his cap or helmet with the finger-tips of his outstretched hand. While the salute lasts the left arm ceases swinging and hangs rigidly and vertically downwards. In this attitude the *inferior* marches past his *superior*, always looking at him with an expression of keen attentiveness.

" After having passed the *superior*, the *inferior* keeps on walking in the saluting attitude, exactly as though the *superior* were a queue of *superiors*, six paces deep. When the distance of six paces has been reached, the salute ends with the same abruptness as it started. The head is thrown forward and the arms resume their normal swinging movement."

I can assure you that the procedure was not less complicated to carry out than it is to understand.

A different form of salute existed for Royalties, and flags when carried. It was called a " Making front " and consisted in remaining transfixed at the approach of Royalty or the flag, and following the progress of the Royalty or the flag with one's head until the object of veneration had reached a point

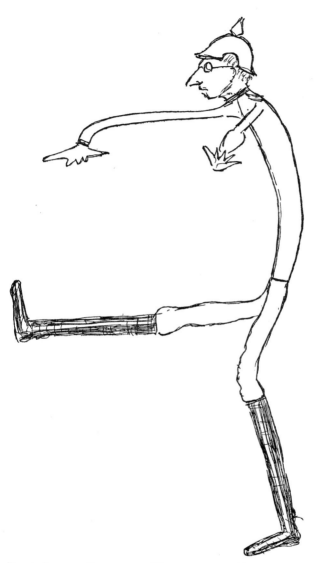

PRINCE LEOPOLD LOEWENSTEIN-WERTHEIM HAD A DIFFICULT WAR.

in one's field of vision corresponding to the natural limit of the revolving radius of one's neck. This form of salute was due to the German Emperor " everywhere," to the King of Bavaria " everywhere, except in Prussia," and to the other federal rulers " within their own territory."

We practised the salute daily, the sergeant-major representing both the approach of the royal carriage and the monarch and testing our alertness by suddenly exclaiming :

" I am the Grand Duke of Baden, but you are Bavarian, and we are at the moment in the Grand Duchy of Oldenburg. Now what are you going to do ? "

Then followed the first lessons in goose-stepping. At first I thought them amusing, as in fact a good many things in military life would be amusing if it were not for the time-honoured principle which holds that if something is done well without the use of invectives, it is bound to be done even better if invectives are freely used.

To stand on one leg while keeping the other suspended in mid-air, the tip of one's foot pointing downwards, and to remain in this position for a few minutes in order to learn the correct sense of equilibrium, is, in itself not so unpleasant ; but to be told, at the slightest sign of muscular tremor that one does it on purpose in order to attract attention, when this is particularly unjustified in view of one's knock-kneed condition, is humiliating and apt to make one feel self-conscious.

I cannot describe the entire movement of the goose-step in detail. Each step consists of five to six different consecutive movements, which, as one progresses in mastering them one by one, merge into one comprehensive evolution into which the goose-stepper must put all that is within him of faith, hope, love, pride, every emotion, high and base, his very soul and life if he wants to produce the right effect. The more standardised the feelings of a nation are, as in war or under a dictatorship, the more perfect the goose-step will be, but those who believe in the freedom of the individual can never hope to be good goose-steppers.

In 1916, when I entered the Cadet Corps, the enthusiasm of the first war years had already vanished. As the colour disappeared from the fields and woods of Europe, battered into grey mud by the opposing armies, colour and joy also left the hearts of men. It was a drab uniformity of death which was gradually engulfing the world. The German military machine still worked with the greatest precision, like a huge monster which spread its tentacles all over the country and into every sphere of life, swallowing more and more of the civilian population and transforming them into parts of its organism. This human " fuel " in 1916 possessed no more the qualities it had in 1914, yet the mechanism of the army was so perfectly constructed that it seemed to matter very little so long as there were still sufficient men to keep it going.

One of the secrets of this organisation was the system of drilling for the sake of drilling. It seemed entirely divorced from the real exigence of the moment and the ultimate task of the soldier on the battlefield. It served, however, a much more important purpose, for it prevented people from thinking and made them so machine-like that they almost failed to notice the difference between goose-stepping across a courtyard and storming a trench. Indeed, the latter form of exercise often appeared to us to be a welcome form of relaxation compared to the one of having to shoulder one's rifle 300 times, just for the sake of timing the three stages of shouldering properly.

After having drilled for about two months without rifles, all those whose muscles seemed strong enough were given rifles, the real army rifles which were extremely heavy. Goose-stepping without rifles is difficult enough, but with a rifle whose butt leaned heavily against one's shoulder and whose muzzle protruded vertically into the sky, it became a feat of acrobatics. I found it quite impossible to co-ordinate all the necessary movements into a harmonious whole. I could either only watch my rifle, in which case my legs got out of control and stepped into each other's path, or I could watch my legs, in which case the rifle would begin to sway on my shoulder, knocking it blue and green. In the rare moments in which I succeeded in mastering both rifle and legs I presented a picture of such utter stiffness and cramp that I could have passed for a cartoon libelling the spirit of the army.

The end of the daily drilling class regularly consisted in having to march past the commandant one by one. Each cadet knew that when he had reached a certain point between the start and the finish he was safe. If he reached this point without having been ordered back, it meant that he had

255

either passed the test to the satisfaction of the officer, or had escaped his notice altogether. He could then continue the march with less effort and return to his quarters. I was one of those unfortunates who were regularly sent back, often three or four times.

Whenever I thought that I had just passed the critical line I heard the piercing shout, " Cadet Loewenstein, back ! " And back I rushed and goose-stepped once more through the open square, and again I was sent back. It was as though the field were divided by an invisible live wire which automatically drove me back whenever I approached it. With each renewed attempt I lost more and more control over myself until, sometimes, completely exhausted, I refused to continue. In order to do so, however, I had to walk up to the commanding officer, stop at a distance of six paces from him and then goose-step three further paces towards him, stand at attention and shout : " I report obediently that I am unable to continue ; I feel ill." I usually looked it and was allowed to retire which, however, did not increase my popularity with the High Command.

Having received a few months' training, we were allowed leave on Sundays. It was then we put on our special uniform which in itself looked quite smart. It was sky blue with black velvet collar and sleeves and white emblems. It is in the nature of things, however, that a smart uniform looks smart on some people, but not on others. It never did on me, at least I don't think so now. If I looked as I felt I looked it might have been different, for I remember distinctly thinking that I looked well and walking through the streets of Munich with the deliberation and nonchalance of one who feels sure of himself. I had my picture taken by a photographer, and it is when looking at this picture now that I know the uniform did not suit me. I was very thin, my face narrowed down to the chin in an elongated triangle, my nose was as big as it is now ; therefore, relatively speaking, much bigger, and my eyes looked melancholic from under the uncouth helmet and behind the flimsy pince-nez (I was not allowed to wear spectacles, they were considered " intellectual " and therefore, unsuited to a soldier). In those days, however, everybody liked the photograph, and even my father commented on it approvingly.

My greatest pride on Sunday was not the uniform but the detachable white cuffs which I had received permission to buy after a protracted correspondence between myself and my father on the one hand, and my father and the company chief on the other.

" You must have white cuffs," my classmates told me, " it is most essential on Sundays when you are invited to drink tea."

" I must have white cuffs," I wrote to my father, who wrote back " Why ? "

" You must also get a greasy hair lotion," the superior told me, " your hair is always dishevelled and your parting crooked " (which it is to the present day).

" I must have a greasy hair lotion," I wrote to my father, who wrote back, " How vulgar ! "

However, I insisted, and my father wrote to the company chief :

" My son informs me that he needs white cuffs and a greasy hair lotion. Should he really need it (please find out, dear Captain), then I will raise no further objections."

I was summoned to the captain, an elderly reserve officer who had been a schoolmaster.

He said : " Cadet . . . What is your name ? "

" Loewenstein."

" Cadet Loewenstein, your father writes that you desire white cuffs and a greasy hair lotion. Is that correct ? "

" Zu Befehl, Herr Hauptmann, most obediently, yes."

" Let me look at your hair, cadet. Yes, it does look disreputable. Don't you ever brush it ? "

" Zu Befehl, Herr Hauptmann, most obediently, I brush it frequently."

" I believe," the captain observed, " your hair is of the kind no amount of brushing will keep down."

" Zu Befehl, Herr Hauptmann, most obediently, to express my opinion I believe it is of that kind."

" Then you shall have your hair lotion."

" Zu Befehl, Herr Hauptmann, thank you most obediently."

" I shall also write to your father that you need the cuffs."

" Thank you most obediently."

That was one of the rare moments when I felt a proud soldier.

There were other moments when I felt humiliated to the point of wishing to commit suicide, and all my nightmares to the present day centre round those moments.

Prince Leopold Loewenstein-Wertheim

When we were sufficiently familiar with the handling of our rifles, we were taken for the first marches across the town and into the open country. I have said before that the rifle was heavy, but not until I went for the first march did I think that it could be too heavy altogether for me. To my unspeakable horror, I noticed after the first ten minutes' marching that my left arm, which held the rifle over my shoulder, was beginning to give way. At first there was an acute pain, then all feeling left it and it just gave way as if it did not belong to me. Not with the greatest effort of will power could I check the decline of my left arm. The rifle slid more and more off my shoulder, and I knew that in another minute I would drop it altogether. The group leader, who had been watching me for some time, resorted to the approved method of insulting me, but quickly realised that no insult could remedy the situation, the rifle was simply too heavy, so, rather than expose the whole corps to the utter disgrace of having a soldier drop his gun, he ran to the officer and whispered something into his ear. Whereupon the latter gave the command to carry the rifles at ease, which meant carrying them in any way one liked. I was nearly fainting at that moment.

Although my arm gradually grew stronger, I had to pass through the same agonising moments again and again until I invented a device which changed me from the worst rifle carrier of the school into its best.

I made myself a sort of wristband with a hook, and as soon as we had shouldered our rifles I hooked

my left arm on the cartridge belt, thus giving it the
support it needed. I could now carry the rifle
shouldered, if need be, for hours, and when the
rifles of others began to sway after a long march,
mine remained steady and vertical. No one suspected what had happened, and the sudden change
in me was generally attributed to the magic of
military discipline, which makes a man out of a
civilian.

The War continued aimlessly. The thought of
peace, which had been present in 1916, was post-
poned *sine die*.

Life seemed as though suspended forever in a
stalemate of death and desolation. There seemed
no hope that it might arise anew.

Against this steadily darkening background we
continued to perform our goose-stepping evolutions
quite oblivious of what was happening around us.
One might almost say we retired into them, as a
Yogi does into his meditations, as the only true
reality in a world of illusion.

Towards the end of 1917 the Cadet Corps
gradually diminished in number. All those who
reached the age of seventeen (later on even sixteen)
went straight to the front, and practically all of them
were killed within the first two weeks of their front
service. To be killed in action immediately on
leaving the school seemed to us the logical con-
clusion of our military training. That there might
exist some different solution (for instance, that the
War might end before long) did not seriously occur
to us.

I was one of the few who reckoned with this

possibility and even anticipated that a war could end with the defeat of Germany.

The thought was not displeasing to me. I was convinced that a lost war would mean the dissolution of the Cadet Corps. " Whatever the outcome of the War," I thought, " I shall accept it. If we win, the victory is worth the sacrifice of remaining at the school. If we lose, the school will be dissolved and my military career will come to an end."

The collapse came suddenly. For us the end came overnight. There was shooting, and in the morning we woke up to hear that Bavaria had been proclaimed a republic. The Cadet Corps was occupied by a red guard to whom we surrendered our rifles, and all military training was stopped.

When my father, who was with the retreating armies in France, received my letter informing him of what had happened and asking him to provide me with civilian clothes, he sent a telegram to the commandant.

" I request," he wired, " that my son should leave the corps, at once, as I have no intention of letting him become an officer in a republican army."

It was a dull, raining December day when I walked out of the gates of the Cadet Corps. The coat of arms above the gates was covered by a red cloth. As I reached the end of the square I heard a distant sound of goose-stepping which came from the group of red soldiers changing guard at the school.

Thus ended my military career.

The First Time I went to New York

by

P. G. WODEHOUSE

THE other day I received a letter from one of
our younger literati, who has gone to America with
the idea of establishing personal contacts, as they
call it, with American publishers and—if the good
old racket has not turned blue by this time—doing
a bit of lecturing. The bulk of the communication
is not of any great interest, dealing as it does
almost entirely with the subject of how good the
writer is, but it ends with a—to me—intensely
significant passage.

As follows :

> " I have placed my affairs on this side in the
> hands of a man named Jake Skolsky. I have
> given him a novel and some short stories to sell.
> He seems very capable and full of enthusiasm."

It electrified me.

" Sweet suffering soupspoons ! " I thought. " Can
it be that old Jake is still alive ? He must be a
hundred. And, if alive, how on earth does he come
to be alive ? Has no one shot him in all this long
time ? It seems incredible."

And, as I mused, the years fell away, hair sprouted
on the vast bare steppes of my head, where never
hair has been almost within the memory of man,

and I was once more a piefaced lad paying my first visit to New York.

Most people bring back certain definite impressions from their first visit to New York. They may be of the serious-minded type that wags its head and says, " What is the future of this great country ? " or they may belong to the whimsical, frivolous brigade and write light essays on the difficulty they had in getting their shoes cleaned at the hotel ; but to whichever class they are affiliated they are sure to speak of towering skyscrapers, majestic skylines, and the American girl.

When I came home, people asked me in vain about these things. I did not remember them. I suppose they were there. No doubt there was a skyline. Even in those days there must have been skyscrapers. And the place, I should imagine, was full of American girls. But I was too preoccupied to notice them. My whole attention throughout my visit was absorbed by Jake Skolsky, the capable and enthusiastic literary agent.

As Nicholas Boileau-Despreaux (1636–1711) says in Bartlett's well-known " Book of Familiar Quotations," " Every age has its pleasures, its style of wit, and its own ways." And, one might add, its own literary agents. It is one of the compensations of advancing years that time seems to bring with it bigger and better literary agents. When you arrive at the stage where the question of Japanese second serial rights crops up, you have generally got somebody looking after your affairs incapable of pocketing a yen. But in one's early days to get paid for the outright sale of a short story was a wonderful adventure. Especially in America, if you were represented by Jake Skolsky.

If this sketch had been written twenty-five years ago, when the blood was hot and the agony of being gypped out of most of one's microscopic income still fresh and raw, I should probably have begun it with the words, "I call on Heaven to judge between this man and me." Or would I? Perhaps not, even then. For all through our association I could never quite bring myself to regard Jake as a fellow human being. He was always just a sort of Thing wriggling on the prismatic surface of New York life.

An old actor once told me of a club which used to exist during Buckstone's days at the Haymarket. At the meetings of the club the members sat round a big barrel, which had a hole in the top. Through this hole they were wont to throw any scraps and odds and ends they did not want. Bits of tobacco, bread, marrow bones, the dregs of their glasses— anything and everything went into the barrel. "And," said my informant, "as the barrel became fuller and fuller, strange animals made their appearance—animals of peculiar shape and form crawled out of the barrel and attempted to escape across the floor. But we headed them off with our sticks, sir, and we chased them back again into the place where they had been born and bred. We poked them in, sir, with our sticks."

Many a time when he was handling my affairs, I used to feel that Jake would have gone back into that barrel. And no questions asked, either, by its inhabitants. Just another of the boys, they would have said to themselves.

My first dealings with Jake were through the medium of the post. It was a medium to which, as I shall show later, he did not always trust, but he did so on this occasion, and very charming letters he wrote. I have lost them now, but I remember them. I had sent the MS. of a novel of mine, "Love Among the Chickens," to an English friend living in New York. Pressure of business compelled him to hand it over to a regular agent. He gave it to Jake. That was the expression he used in writing to me—"I am giving it to Jake Skolsky"—and I think Jake must have taken the word "giving" literally. Certainly, when the book was published in America, it had on its title page, "Copyright by Jacob Skolsky," and a few years later, when the story was sold for motion pictures, I was obliged to pay Jake two hundred and fifty dollars to release it.

For the book was published in America. I will say that for Jake—he sold not only the book rights but the serial rights, and at a price which seemed to me fantastic. A thousand dollars it was, and to one who, like myself, had never got above fifty pounds for a serial and whose record royalties for a book were eighteen pounds eleven and fourpence, a thousand dollars was more than merely good. It was great gravy. It made the whole world seem different. A wave of gratitude towards my benefactor swept over me. I felt like a man who has suddenly got in touch with a rich and benevolent uncle.

There was just one flaw in my happiness. The

money seemed a long time coming. In the letter (a delightful letter) in which he informed me of the sale, Jake said that a draft would arrive on October 1st. But October came and went. "These busy New Yorkers," I said to myself. "They have so little time. I must be patient." By Christmas I was inclined to restlessness. In March I cabled, and received a reply, "Letter explaining. Cheque immediately." Late in April the old restlessness returned, for no explaining letter had arrived. Towards the middle of May I decided to go to New York. In several of his letters Jake had told me I was the coming man. I came.

Jake entered my life heralded by a cloud of smoke and the penetrating aroma of one of the most spirited young cigars I have ever encountered ; a little vulture-like man with green eyes, yellow hands, a blue suit, a red tie, and grey hair. Quite a colour scheme he presented that pleasant May morning.

"Say, listen," said Jake.

It was an interesting story that he told. Sad, too. It seemed that where he had gone wrong was in trying to kill two birds with one stone. There was a charming girl of his acquaintance whom he wanted me to meet, and he also wanted me to get my cheque. And as this girl was leaving for England, the happy idea struck him to give her the cheque to take to me. By doing this, he would avoid all chance of having the letter get lost in the post and would enable his friend to meet me in circumstances where she would catch me at my best and sunniest—

viz., while fingering a cheque for a thousand dollars.

But what he had failed to take into account was that she would visit Monte Carlo on her way to England . . .

There being no Southern route in those days, this surprised me a little.

" Monte Carlo ? " I said.

" Monte Carlo," said Jake.

" Monte *Carlo ?* " I said.

" Monte Carlo," said Jake.

" But I didn't know . . ."

" Say, listen," said Jake.

He resumed his story. Yes, she had stopped off at Monte Carlo *en route*. But even then, mind you, it would have been all right if she had been by herself. She was a nice girl, who would never have dreamed of cashing a stranger's cheque. But her brother was with her, and he had fewer scruples. He gambled at the tables and lost ; borrowed his sister's jewellery, and lost again. After that, there was nothing left for him to do but fall back on my cheque.

" But don't you worry," said Jake, so moved, I remember, that he forgot to begin, " Say, listen." " You shall be paid. I will pay you myself. Yessir ! "

And he gave me ten dollars and told me to get my hat and come along and see editors.

Jake had magnetism. In his presence I was but as a piece of chewed string. There were moments before we separated when I almost believed that story and thought it rather decent of him to let me have ten dollars. Ten dollars, I meant to say . . .

just like that . . . right out of his own pocket. Pretty square.

His generalship was, I admit, consummate. He never ceased to keep moving. All that day we were dashing into elevators, dashing out, plunging into editorial offices ("Shake hands with Mr. Wodehouse"), plunging out, leaping into street cars, leaping out, till anything like rational and coherent thought was impossible.

He made only one tactical error. That was when he introduced me to the man to whom he had given my cheque.

He was an author from Kentucky. His experience had been practically identical with mine. He had sent his stories from Kentucky to a friend in New York, and the friend had handed them on to Jake, and Jake had sold them with magical skill, and then there had occurred that painful stage-wait in the matter of the cashing up. Eventually, when he was about twelve hundred dollars down, the author, breathing hot Southern maledictions, packed a revolver and started for New York.

I think Jake must have been a little out of sorts the morning they met. The best he could do in the way of a story was to say he had lost the money on Wall Street. Later, he handed the Kentuckian the cheque he had received from the magazine for my novel, asserting that he had sent me another for the same amount.

I did not see that there was anything to be done. New York at that time was full of men who did not see that there was anything to be done about Jake. He was so friendly about it all. When unmasked, he betrayed none of the baffled fury of the stage villain. He listened to you, and considered the matter with his head on one side, like a vulture accused of taking an eyeball to which it was not entitled.

" Why, say, yes," he would observe at length. " Say, listen, I want to have a talk with you about that some time."

You then intimated that there was no time like the present. You pressed him. You were keen and resolute. And then somehow—for the life of you you could not say how—you found all of a sudden that the subject of your wrongs had been shelved and that you were accepting with every sign of goodfellowship a poisonous cigar from his waistcoat pocket.

Yes, Jake had magnetism. Clients might come in upon him like lions, but they always went out like lambs. Not till they had been out from under the influence for a good hour or so did the realisation of their imbecile weakness smite them, and then it was too late. His office, when they revisited it, was empty. He was out somewhere, dashing into elevators, dashing out, plunging into editorial offices, plunging out, leaping into street cars, leaping out. And if by some miracle you did get hold of him, he just stuck his head on one side.

" Why, say, yes . . ."

And all the weary round started again.

Only one man ever got the better of Jake. And he, oddly enough, was not one of the tough story-writers who were or had been reporters, but a poet.

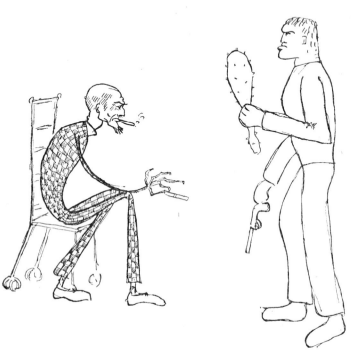

AUTHORS CAME IN UPON JAKE SKOLSKY LIKE LIONS, BUT
THEY ALWAYS LEFT LIKE LAMBS.

Those were the days when New York magazines had rather a weakness for short, crisp, uplift poems calling on the youth of America to throw out its chest and be up and doing. They would print these on their front page, facing the table of contents, accompanied by pictures of semi-nude men with hammers or hoes or whatever it might be, and a magician like Jake could get a hundred dollars out of them per poem.

He had got a hundred dollars for one of this man's poems, and he gave him his cheque for it, less the customary agent's fee. The poet presented the cheque, and it came back marked "Insufficient funds."

You would have said that there was nothing to be done. Nor, in the case of a prose writer, would there have been. Undoubtedly I or my Kentucky friend or any of the rest of Jake's stable would have treated the thing as a routine situation and handled it in the routine way, going round to see Jake—more as a matter of form than anything—and watching him put his head on one side and proceeding through the "Why, say, yes" to the orthodox cigar.

But not the poet. He gave Jake's office boy two dollars to nose about among Jake's papers and find out what his balance at the bank was. Having discovered that it was $73.50, he paid in $26.50 to Jake's account without delay, presented the cheque again, and cleaned Jake out. Jake never really got over that. He said it wasn't the money so much, it was the principle of the thing. It hurt him, the deceitfulness of it in a man on whom he had always looked almost as a son.

There are moments, when I am feeling particularly charitable, when I fancy that it was in that relationship that Jake regarded all of us bright young men. I think he meant well. He knew the temptations which New York holds for the young when they have money in their pockets, and he shielded us from them. What he would really have liked would have been to hold a sort of paternal patriarchal position to his clients. He owned at that time—perhaps he owns it still—what he called a farm down on Staten Island. It looked as if there had once been a house there and somebody had pulled it down and left the tool shed, and he was very urgent in inviting each new client to live at this curious residence.

His ideal, I believe, was to have the place full of eager young men, all working away at their stories and running to him when they wanted a little pocket money. He would have charge of all the cash accruing from their writings and would dole it out bit by bit as needed. Up to the moment when he and I parted for ever he had succeeded in inducing few authors to see eye to eye with him in this matter.

Just after I had written the above, another letter arrived from my friend in America.

" I am having a little trouble with Jake Skolsky," he writes. " He is unquestionably an excellent man and has sold a number of my things, but I find it extraordinarily difficult to get the money from him. However, I have written him a note, informing him that unless he pays up I must place the matter

THE ONLY MAN WHO EVER GOT THE BETTER OF
MR. JACOB SKOLSKY.

in the hands of a lawyer, so I expect things will shortly adjust themselves."

It sounds all right, I own. On the surface it has all the appearance of being a clincher. But, unless the years have played havoc with the old pep and reduced him to a mere shell of the man he used to be, Jake will wriggle out of it somehow. He will see that lawyer and bring his magnetism into play. He will talk to him. He will give him a near-cigar. I should not be surprised if, before the interview is over, he does not borrow money from him.

Sometimes I wonder if I ought to have warned my friend when I got that first letter of his. Thinking it over, I fancy not. He is a young man at the outset of his career, and there is no question of the value of an association with Jake in the formative years of an author's life. Mine was the making of me. Critics to-day sometimes say that my work would be improved by being less morbid, but nobody has ever questioned its depth. That depth I owe to Jake. (He owes me about two thousand dollars.)

The First Time I Met the Team

by

THEODORA BENSON

FOURTEEN is perhaps an odd number for a team. It is excessive for bridge or even cricket and inadequate for football, it is redundant for one eight and stinted for two. It does very well, however, for nuts in May or oranges and lemons, and I think that it has done very well—thirteen of it at any rate—for making a book.

I did not, of course, meet this team for the first time all at one fell swoop, in a sublime, compact gathering. One by one they drifted into my life as the years slipped by. Or did they? There is, of course, the rather moot occasion of the first time that I had the pleasure of meeting Mr. Howard Spring.

It happened quite recently. I found myself sitting next him at a dinner party. On my other side was a particularly charming barrister, but business first. And perhaps pleasure with it, for I rather liked this Mr. Spring. He had an intelligent, sensitive face and nice hands. There were no name cards and my hostess was an indistinct introducer, so I started by making sure that he knew who I was. He did. He knew not only my name, but what I had written, had read a couple of my books, and liked them.

I told him about the novel I was writing. He was interested. We got on like a house on fire. I was

283

quite thrilled and took no notice at all of the
barrister, for I had visions of being chosen for the
Evening Standard book of the month. I have never
quite outgrown the childish feeling that such
distinctions can be in great part won by waggling
the eyelashes or making a felicitous quotation. So
I fairly bust myself, and because I felt myself
successful I was, to two people at any rate, myself
and my quarry, charming. I enjoyed it.

Well, I had the pleasure of meeting Mr. Howard
Spring, but not exactly the meeting. My neighbour
at dinner turned out to be an agreeable Mr.
Howell King.

In a different way, I have never had any
particular first meeting with Miss Rose Macaulay,
although I am happy to say that I know her, and
that, what is more, she knows me. This pleasant
state of affairs—I find it very pleasant—has flowered
gradually and imperceptibly out of many vague,
casual encounters at literary cocktail parties ; which
gives an unjustly piteous impression of the lives we
both lead.

Then, though the idea sounds coy and whimsical,
I might quite well have had, but did not have, a
definite first meeting with myself. There might
have been some recalled moment of very early
childhood when the thought came vividly to me
for the first time : " This is I myself and nobody
else in the world that am making a nice smooth
dust castle at the side of this road in the sun. I am
distinct from everybody else. Baby is me." But
no such memory comes trotting along into the light
of day.

My first encounters with the remaining eleven members of the team (cricket after all) I can remember perfectly.

The first time that I met Betty Askwith was a complete and rounded off occasion. It was the only one of the first meetings that was. It was like a very primitive early lesson from " Psychology Without Tears." One Sunday in London when I was thirteen, my mother said to me :

" Theodora, a very, very great friend of mine is bringing her little girl to tea to-day, and we do hope very much that you two are going to like each other. So do try and be very nice to Betty and not be rough or anything dreadful, won't you ? "

Or words to that effect. Certainly no more. And if I had not been warned I daresay I should have sulked. So what could a parent do ? But I was seldom in the best of moods anyway on a London Sunday afternoon, for we used to be At Home and I used to appear for tea (a gallant attempt to civilise me), which meant my having to be changed and cleaned and tidied and not make a great racket, and I was nervous because of my genius for spilling things.

" How old is this Betty ? " I asked suspiciously. " Well," apologised my poor mother, " she is ten. But only children are generally old for their ages." I tried to sneer, and succeeded, I take it, in looking rather *farouche*.

Meanwhile Betty's mother was saying, " Don't make quite such a fuss about coming out to tea with my friends, darling. You have to meet people sometimes and there's really no sense in being so sure you'll hate Theodora. Three years is *not* a big difference ; no, she is *not* twice your age." (Thank you, Lady Askwith, thank you.)

Well, we met in the drawing-room at my parents' house, both of us looking very good and sweet. Of course, I did not care what Betty looked like, but I have a vivid recollection of my own appearance because I had made such difficulties over it. Hair, fair, slightly fluffy at the ends, cut in a fringe and flowing loose on my shoulders. A grey velvet dress with a thin corduroy stripe and a yoke. A necklace of silver cherubs' heads. A sweet-child-angel-looking face. We were tactfully pushed off into the boudoir to get to know each other. And it is pleasant to recall that we were very fairly civil for a quarter of an hour. As to liking one another, the possiblity of this fantastic contingency was not even considered by either of us.

And then another mamma called upon mine, towing her little boy. I knew him well. He was about Betty's age and exceedingly handsome. They pushed him into the boudoir. He greeted us both rousingly and announced what he wanted to play.

The presence of mind with which Betty instantly snubbed him, the relentless insight with which she'd summed him up in one, made me gasp with admiration. She looked at me to gauge my feelings for him and caught the hate-light shining in my eyes. He was a bumptious boy, and we didn't really manage to give him hell, but I think he was a bit shaken by the time his mother took him away.

My Sister and I Laughed.

By the time her mother took her away, my alliance with Betty was assured.

A year or two later I met Arthur Bryant for the first time, though he and my elder brother and sister were already old friends—indeed she had used to visit them at their prep. school. On this occasion Betty had come to tea with me, and so had a little Russian princess who did lessons with me, and my sister was there, and also an attractive young man in the Foreign Office, who had not come for my bright eyes, as it struck me. And Arthur Bryant turned up as we were playing bears or something, and Betty and I sized him up as quickly as she had the little boy that Sunday, and roped him instantly in upon our side. It was a confused afternoon. The Russian princess, chasing me in a friendly spirit round and round the dining-room table with a carving knife, got so wild and excited that soon I was running absolutely terrified for my life. Arthur Bryant got tied on to the top of the service lift with skipping ropes and told for some reason to howl, which he did like a good one. During hide and seek the young blade in the Foreign Office, tearing down a tiny, tucked-away, illogical flight of stairs from one bedroom to another, fell into a basin of water. And then there was no more frolic. For, of course, my sister and I laughed. And, of course, he thought we'd put the basin there on purpose, and indeed its position is a mystery. No one in their senses would have put it there unless as a booby trap, and yet it was a real accident, for which we were not responsible. He was furious at appearing ridiculous before my sister, and the more dignified he became in his wet trousers the more we laughed. At last, in spite of apologies, protestations of innocence, and cooing, he stamped out of the house in a fury. He lived to speak to us again, but never to forgive. So Arthur Bryant comforted us more than ably by taking us to the " Beggar's Opera " at Hammersmith. He assured us truthfully that any time he fell into a basin of water we would be at liberty to laugh.

I was a really young authoress when I first met Beverley Nichols, I had published only one novel and he had certainly never heard of it. There was, however, a young man, no, a boy, who had read it five times and pasted a newspaper photograph of me on the fly leaf and who was really and truly PROUD of having got to know me. He was a pleasant pink and white boy with blue eyes and yellow curly hair. He wanted to write and I was all the literary lion that he had. One day, however, he called on me in a gentle perspiration of triumph. He had got to know Beverley Nichols.

I was very envious, but had a sort of second-hand share in the triumph. I remember that the two of us composed a mock fan poem for Beverley and felt pretty nonchalant at knowing better than to write him a real one. And then one day this boy did a very generous thing. On one of the rare occasions when he actually went to see Mr. Nichols (though with no appointment) he took me with him.

I spent a long time trying to achieve a really sophisticated appearance. I put on my smartest dress and my best hat. I struggled with cosmetics

I Took Pains to look Smart and Sophisticated and We Started
Off to Call on Mr. Beverley Nichols.

and dabbed on scent. I was satisfied that I looked
knowing and worldly at the end of it.

We were welcomed most charmingly. We were
amusingly and very kindly made to feel ourselves
successes. We left enchanted with our host. The
boy wrote him an immense letter on literature
afterwards and asked at the end of it what he had
thought of me. And a letter of a more reasonable
length patiently answered it. It admitted that
Mr. Nichols had nothing against literature. It
asked a little wistfully if the boy had given up his
plan of going home to Devonshire to write. And it
said, so far as I can remember : " Of course your
friend is charming. It was nice in London to see
anyone looking so fresh and like a milkmaid. She
ought to smell of honey and cowslips, and always
wear that large, childish hat ! "

I think I minded most of all about my hat.
Really it is amazing that after only four years of
embitterment on my side we became most happily
friends.

When I first met Mr. P. G. Wodehouse I had read
every book he had ever published, and all except
those about Ukridge I had loved. I could quote
him by the hour. And not only could. On this
occasion I pretty well did. Charmed with finding
a man such as one could really talk to and who,
moreover, was bound to be well up in one of my
favourite subjects, I gave him an immense lecture on
the works of Mr. P. G. Wodehouse. I was only about
sixteen, and it is not surprising that he was much too
nice to resent it. What surprises me is that on
finding there was nothing else I wanted to talk about

he took the trouble to talk about his work with intelligence and interest. He defended Ukridge against my attacks quite eagerly and yet impersonally. " Yes, I know there is that school of thought. But I do really think that it is wrong." And I was able to let my admiration flow without blushing for it after.

I do not see Mr. Wodehouse very often. But I know no author to whom I could so easily say when I did see him, exactly what I had thought of his last book. My admiration has even deepened since that first time and that is saying a great deal. But if it were a book about Ukridge I should still be vexed.

The first time I met Mr. William Gerhardi I was fascinated by his mind and disappointed by his behaviour. I had studied his books and was prepared to find him Don Juan with the lid off—and persevering too.

It didn't go according to schedule. True he did once or twice let fall some such words as : " I must not see any more of you. It is too disturbing to my peace of mind," or " I wish you were not so beautiful. It is so upsetting to fall in love," but he said these things either in an automatic way with his eyes straying absentmindedly across the room, or as one who is grimly determined to do his duty no matter how little he likes it. I was mystified and rather cross. But even at that first meeting the pleasure of long, long future talks was foreshadowed. Even then the utterly unforeseen occurred. We liked each other.

William Gerhardi was responsible for my first meeting with Prince Leopold Loewenstein-Wertheim and with Mr. Hugh Kingsmill. These were two separate occasions.

Betty Askwith and I had asked him round one evening, and he had asked if he might bring a friend. I was staying at Betty's house, and I remember that we told the parlourmaid with pride that we were expecting two gentlemen at about 9 o'clock and would she put for them whisky and soda and sandwiches, and that at 10 o'clock she asked in a very mortifying way if she shouldn't clear away the tray. But at 10.30 Mr. Gerhardi and Prince Loewenstein arrived, and when we all realised that it was 4 a.m. they went away again.

We found them both the most delightful conversationalists, intellectual, very amusing, sometimes oddly inspiring. But I remember most vividly that Prince Loewenstein had hay fever and that this reminded him to tell us a story about a time when he had had hay fever and had been in love. It was a long story, without much pattern or climax, and I suppose it was just a case of " only, of course, dear, it isn't so much what he says, you know, it's the way he says it." I have never heard a more brilliantly told story. Often at dark moments I long to be told it again, even if it had to be without the enhancement of Prince Loewenstein having hay fever at the time of telling. But it was a nebulous story and he has forgotten it. He has even told me others all but as good since. It was absorbing and utterly dispassionate. The only bit I actually remember concerns a verbal attack of the utmost ferocity made upon him by an infuriated Frenchman.

" Only look at yourself ! " yelled this enemy derisively at the end of it.

" And I looked at myself," said Prince Loewenstein, " and I thought my boots, yes, they were a little too new and yellow, and my waistcoat, well, it was rather a mistake, and my tie, perhaps it was on the loud side, and all the time I was overpowered with my hay fever. I could not help beginning to see his point of view. It struck me as possible that he might be right . . ."

Mr. Hugh Kingsmill, on the other hand, would not, I felt at our first meeting, have been in the least shaken by anything the Frenchman said. He had a very good technique in argument of interpreting you to yourself in a sadly vain and futile light, with so much sympathy and tolerance that you almost accepted it. Your denials and protests worked against you as when madmen will opine that they are sane.

William Gerhardi, Betty Askwith, Mr. Kingsmill, my sister and I were dining together for " Othello " at the Old Vic. Mr. Kingsmill had been warned about Betty and myself, but my sister came as a surprise to him and he kept nudging William and asking him perfectly audible questions about her age, her habits, her husband and her children, none of which he was able to answer. There couldn't be anyone better than Hugh Kingsmill to go to a Shakespeare play with. He loved it so really and truly, and yet was often so frivolous about it, whispering in the middle, for instance, that Cassio was plainly an old Harrovian. He talked tremendously and well. He not only said good things, but, better still, drew us girls out to say them.

We went back to my flat to talk afterwards, but we dropped my sister at her home on the way. The men protested. I suggested airily that old Othello would be waiting up to strangle her, as she had got the most frightfully jealous husband. " Has she really got a jealous husband ? " they asked with interest.

" Oh, yes," said Betty, " *and* he's black."

A very great friend of mine, Alan Pryce-Jones, once asked me to lunch, at the Ritz, and as though that were not a sufficient treat he produced **Mr.** Evelyn Waugh to meet me.

This was a noble thought, as few had (or have) a higher opinion of Mr. E. Waugh's work than I have. And I enjoyed the occasion immensely. The only sad thing was that the treat to some extent misfired because I did not hear Mr. Waugh's name at the time of introduction.

They were both very amusing, but whereas Alan said witty things in ordinary English, Mr. E. Waugh said them in the limited though expressive vocabulary of a preparatory school for boys. I thought it nice and unaffected of me and Alan to perceive that this unliterary chump had an odd charm to him.

I found out who he was after meeting him again at some gathering ; where I had gone up to him, I remember, with a view to patronising him. He did not seem to resent this attention. But all the same it can't be done.

And now, scanning again the list of Fourteen Varieties with which this book very honestly begins,

I notice the names of Miss Dorea Stanhope, and Miss Antonia White ; and I wonder why, as editor, with unlimited powers at any rate of veto, I even considered nursing these two serpents in my bosom. Which is what it amounts to, for I have promised in writing to pay them something, and the printer has set them up in the same sized type as anybody else.

Take Miss Antonia White. You might think to look at her that she was very nice, and for all I really know you would be quite right. I met her once a few months ago, and have only seen her for about five seconds since. At the time of meeting her I do not remember having ever seen a photograph of her, that is to say that I did not know her by sight. I knew that she had written a very successful book called " Frost in May," but I had not read it, and I had read and liked and laughed over a brilliant essay of hers. We met at a party.

I arrived alone at this party, which took place in a house in Chelsea that was decorated and furnished from roof to ground floor (I have not seen the basement) in unbroken good taste without being in the least antagonising. It was a nice party and very gay. It was a special brand of gaiety, not in the least a romp, but light and crystalline and tenuous like a beautiful big soap bubble floating about and bouncing slightly. Everyone was well groomed, and many of them good-looking, and there was an atmosphere of witty things being said just out of hearing.

Perhaps you can see from this why I did not, on finding myself unnoted and unloved, immediately go home. Who minds occasionally not enjoying a party when there is the beautiful compensation of going early to bed? They are rather a toss up anyway if one has not made a date with anybody. If one is bored or harassed it is a social duty to go before one's face reveals it or one's heart harbours unthankfulness. But this looked the sort of party that I could and should enjoy, and I wanted to enjoy it. So I stayed and was introduced to ships that passed in the night, and I ate vast quantities of a chocolate cream sweet that was in itself worth double the cost of my taxi drive to the party.

Then I found an anchor, for there arrived a most personable young gentleman who knew, and did not seem to mind it, nobody else but me. He was tall and strong with broad shoulders and fair curly hair and one of those jaws. Suitable descriptions leap to my pen—steel grey eyes with a glint of laughter, whimsical mouth, long, lithe frame, and even (I suppose) faultless evening dress. You understand that he looked as though he preferred strangling grizzlies with rattlesnakes to flirting in ballrooms, but could do both equally well if he cared to try. Also that I was rather proud of him.

Very soon he began to tell me how that many people envied him, but that really he had a strangely difficult and unhappy life. Everything was just a matter of temperament, wasn't it? Now, take his temperament. . . . I composed my spirit for a happy evening. For this, oddly enough, is what I like. Even if I never get a fair turn myself at all. Even though with the talker it only assigns me the position of good old Theo, a damned sensible

woman. It is not that I remember any of it afterwards or could, even if I would, use it as " copy "
as lay people suppose writers to call it—and suppose
perfectly correctly for the matter of that. (Though,
indeed, Us Authors never look for " copy " or think
about it at all. We have far too much of it. It
droppeth as the gentle rain from heaven. What we
would look for if we were not too lazy would be
plots. And look in vain, and look in vain.) It is
not a thirst for private details, or a yearning to be
confided in, for indeed the thing that soothes and
charms me most of all is to have two men talk
across me about their work. No matter how dreary
and technical the thing may be. It is simply that
what drink is to some of these fourteen authors,
drugs to others, blackmail and arson to the rest, so
to me is listening to men talking about themselves.

Naturally I tried to secure fair play.

" Now that's interesting," I said, " for with me
it works exactly the other way. What I always
feel is . . ."

" Ah, but then I had such a peculiar upbringing,"
he struck in. " Did I ever tell you, to begin with,
that my mother was a nonconformist ? "

I could not remember that he had, although I
felt that he must have many times.

" My father," I interrupted eagerly, " is a . . ."

Here I paused, for I had been about to say a
Mohammedan, and it now struck me that this was
untrue. My predicament gave him his chance.
He brushed my whole family aside.

" Look here," he said generously, " I'll give you
the whole position. Where's a quiet place to sit

My Young Man Gaped at Miss Antonia White.

down ? " And at that innocently happy moment his eyes fell upon Miss Antonia White.

" Who's that girl ? " he asked, in a low voice.

" I don't know," said I.

" It's Antonia White," said a girl who had been towed up and introduced to him and was still hovering around.

" I would like to meet her," said he.

I wasn't going to have the hovering girl butting in. If he'd got to be introduced to Miss Antonia White, I could do it myself, for though I did not know her we had contributed to the same volume of essays, and, of course, wanted to make sure that we had been paid the same amount. I scooped her in, and very nice to me she was, and I introduced my personable young gentleman. After which he brushed me aside as he had earlier and conversationally brushed aside my father.

I did not mind. " Let them enjoy themselves," I thought, full of good will, and returned to the rather voluptuous charms of the chocolate cream sweet.

What stung was this. A little later I noticed him still with her. She was talking to two other young men and he hung on the outskirts gawping at her. She left him to it. My masculine masterpiece, my one buck lamb that she had taken from me, plainly aroused no interest in her at all.

He saw me home, but I was so cross and mortified that although he began in the taxi about his early passion for fretwork, I fell asleep.

And then take Miss Dorea Stanhope. I met her also for the first time, and indeed so far for the last time, at a party. And what a party ! That was a romp if you like—and as it happened I did like. It was also some years ago, so that I have to gaze back through the mists of time and the fumes of drink (for it was a highly successful bottle party) to get my picture.

I arrived at it one of a party of six. The band consisted of Miss Stanhope and Co., " the Bandits." However, our reactions were not at all " Good God, a female band ! Let's go to the ' Berkeley.' " Quite apart from the fact that the " Berkeley " was some eighty-six miles away, the Bandits looked kind of chic and snappy and as though they had ample justification for playing hot music. There were pink coats and a wilderness of bottles and it was a proper frolic.

There were, I remember, a great many emotional and other cross currents, and wheels, if I may say so, within wheels. Yet all these were submerged by the high tide of unbridled party spirit (those wheels and bridles are not quite right in my synthetic seascape). There was a slippery middle-aged man in whom at the moment I took a rather more than maternal interest which he reciprocated warmly as a part of his polygamous outlook on life. There were rivals and mischief-makers. And my charmer was immensely taken with Miss Dorea Stanhope. But she, after all, was safely tethered to a piano, drum, bassoon or what not. And what, anyway, of anything ? It was A Party.

My charmer deserted me for a towheaded baby. I found someone I liked who danced far better than he. Later on at the buffet my charmer and the towheaded baby rushed up to us, and we four began to sing pre-war and war-time songs, moving on (as no one seemed to mind) to a few post-war masterpieces. After we had woken up some rather glazed and static people at the buffet, we thought we would sing our best piece, which was called " Sweet Child," to Miss Stanhope. This was partly in order to give her pleasure, and partly with the idea that the Bandits might afterwards play it, and that we four should disentangle and dance. You know foxtrot choruses. You know how there is a bit in the middle that is different from the rest and comparatively tricky. I was the only one who was really certain and confident about that section of " Sweet Child." The other three sang it all over the place. After the second repetition Miss Stanhope hushed the others for these few lines, and the next three times I sang them as a solo.

> " I'm gonna say to each fellow that I meet,
>   Say, by the way, that's my baby, ain't she
>   sweet . . ."

Good words, you see, and an excellent tune. Then I made a jarring discovery. Miss Stanhope had not promoted me because she thought my rendering better than that of my three friends. She thought it more excruciatingly funny. It is the injustice that rankles. For I always sang " Sweet Child," and do to this day, with accuracy and taste, as anyone can find out for themselves by asking me for a demonstration.

And where did I meet Louis Golding for the first time ? Also at a party (" Oh, Nina, *what a lot of parties.*") It was an enormous party full of authors and actors and publishers and literary agents and artists, but particularly authors. The standard of looks was rather low, the standard of conversation was excellent, and the doings were fine. Alec Waugh, a very old, and for the matter of that a very valued acquaintance of mine, introduced to me Louis Golding. And what follows is very odd. I remember it perfectly. Louis Golding said to me in the strongest possible north-country accent :

" Are yer Cha-agford ? "

And I, hypnotised by the accent, replied : " Noa, A-alec's Cha-agford." Meaning that Alec was one of the young authors who often went down to write in peace at a certain inn at a Devonshire village, and that I was not.

Now I have seen Louis Golding constantly since, and I have never heard him speak with the faintest suggestion of a north-country accent. Also he protests that at the time he had never heard of Chagford and that the entire episode is impossible. I see this. My own explanation is that by some psychic and psychological fact I got into direct communication with his soul. His is that I am a poor muddle-headed liar.